Softly Awakes My Heart

Terry Parker

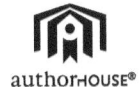

authorHOUSE®

AuthorHouse™ UK Ltd.
500 Avebury Boulevard
Central Milton Keynes, MK9 2BE
www.authorhouse.co.uk
Phone: 08001974150

This book is a work of non-fiction. Unless otherwise noted, the author and the publisher make no explicit guarantees as to the accuracy of the information contained in this book and in some cases, names of people and places have been altered to protect their privacy.

First published by AuthorHouse 1/7/2010

ISBN: 978-1-4490-6797-7 (sc)

This book is printed on acid-free paper.

This is a true story about love at first sight; it happened to a middle-aged couple who fell in love and became an inspired partnership, which led to a loving marriage. In their small exhibition stand and graphic design studio, they worked hard together through the ups and downs that all businesses go through.

When down, their love, comfort, and togetherness got them over these problems. When up, they enjoyed themselves in the fast lane, like a couple of young lovers, kissing, cuddling, and dancing the night away. Their world was wonderful, such happiness, such togetherness, such love.

But in November 2008, their whole world changed.

How did it all start, Tel?

Here I am, sitting in the Crem, with my Gary on one side, my Terrie on the other, and Debbie behind with my lovely little Suzie. I haven't really known her, as I left the family home and got divorced when Suzie was only eight. The most wonderful lady in my life is in the oak box in front of me, and I'm crying my heart out, wondering how I will ever cope. I just don't know.

What a bitch life is. When you think you're on top, something comes along and tries to pull you down. I can, as an old bloke, see sometimes why some folk go on drugs or become alcoholics. Yes before I met my Margaret, I was very near to becoming an alcoholic myself; it's so easy to become one. It's so very hard to kick it – yes, I know.

Friends say, "Be strong, think of all the great times you have had." Yes, I will. I have wonderful memories of our happiness together, but the memories are no substitute for cuddles with my Margaret.

Initially, I wanted to be a carpenter when I left school, but at 13 years, I got a Royal Academy gold medal for a painting, so I decided to become a commercial artist. When I left school, I worked in an advertising agency in London as a messenger boy, then I went into to the studio to learn to become a commercial artist. I was called up for nation service 1954.

In 1956, after I came out of the army I ignored the job that I could have returned to after national service. Instead, I went and worked in my dad's pub in Islington. My dad was a hard man to work for, but the only thing I didn't like was the way the public treated you – no manners, no please or thank you. But I carried on. Coming out of the army, I didn't find it to be any problem.

An Irish couple came in the pub at the weekends with their daughter who I quite liked. This young girl was a very lovely young lady, and we started going out together. We were happy together, and one thing led to another. The little lady started to put on weight, and when this type of mistake happened in the 50s, gentlemen did the right thing. We got married in December 1957, and the young lady was disowned by her parents. We found a top-floor, furnished two-room flat in Dalston, and I packed up working in my dad's pub in Islington and got a job in a brewery.

On 2 June 1958, at 9.30 a.m., I got a phone call that my wife had gone into labour. At 10.20 a.m., she had a wonderful little girl, our Terrie.

Some time later, I left the brewery because of shift work and went to work at BDH, British Drug Houses. Now, don't laugh; I left the BDH because I started to develop breasts. If you worked on a drug called Stilbestrol, a drug for women, and didn't wear a mask, yes – you would get tits.

I then went working on the roads with a paddy gang who came in Dad's pub; I took the 5.30 a.m. train to Guilford every day and did piece work (paid by the yard). Then got a job driving a dumper truck and looking after all the machines on a building site. This was OK, as it wasn't such an early start, and I was happy. By this time, we had two kids, and all was well. But then we were rained off, no work. So I was very worried – no money. Then the general foreman said to me, "You're a bit of an artist… I know a bloke who has a display company whose sign writer has just died, and he needs a writer; can you do it?" Being out of work also getting back into a trade similar to that I loved and started off wanting to do I said yes.

I made an appointment to see the owner of the small display company. He had an urgent sign job to be done, so he didn't have much choice. He asked me when I could do it, and I told him that I was rained off and could start straight away. The job took just over a day and half. The boss was well pleased and paid me for two days' work. I then asked him if there was any chance of a full-time job. He thought about it then said, "Yes, can you start next week?"

I thanked him and told him, "No problem."

At last, I was back in the trade full-time. At the little display firm, I learnt how to spray panels and silkscreen printing. I did a lot of work on animated displays. After a couple of months, I got myself a little car, which made things a lot easier in getting to work and taking out the wife and kids,

The boss of the display company also owned a music hall with his brother, and they used put on still-lady nude shows. At the shows, when the curtains were fully closed, my boss or his brother went on the stage, licked his fingers, then pulled the nipples of the models to make them stick out. As soon this was OK, he got off the stage, and the curtains were pulled back for all to see. Then the curtains were closed, the ladies went into another position, they got their nipples pulled again, and the curtains were opened. This went on for about two hours. Then the ladies and the owners went down to the bar for drinks, and a good time was had by all.

After about a year, I saw a job advertised for a silk screen printer in a big company. I was more money and closer to home, so I went for an interview and got the job. After a day, the boss said there was a post in the layout studio and he had looked at my background, so he asked if I would like it. I was so, so pleased to get back on a drawing board again. The work involved doing layouts for large and small posters – the type used in supermarkets. The layouts would then go to the stencil-cutting room. The stencils were then cut and given to the printer, who would then iron them on the silk, ready for printing.

But again I got itchy feet, and I saw a job advertised in Watford for an exhibition stand designer in a display and exhibition contracting company, so I thought I would give it a go. I met the studio manager, but as I had no exhibition stand drawings or pictures, he asked me to go away and do a block plan, elevations, and a coloured visual of a stand and bring it back to him to see. This I did, but he wasn't very happy. He said to me, "You have never designed an exhibition stand in your life. Why should I give you a job?"

I told him that I would work hard and learn. I also told him I had a wife and three kids. The studio manager just sat and looked at me for about five minutes, puffed on his fag, and said, "If I take you on would you take home work every evening that I set you to teach and train you?" Of course my answer was yes. When I got the job, we moved to a ground and basement flat just off the Holloway road, round the corner to the arsenal football ground with a very nice old couple living above us.

This was new side of my art – exhibition stand design. It was hard to work all day and then work in the evening and to drive to Watford and back to London every day. The exhibition trade is like show biz: the show must go on. I designed a big double-decker stand for a well-known building company. First, after the design had been accepted and I was doing the work drawings, the client decided to reduce their space size. This was not a real problem, as I just had to alter the drawing details a little. But when I arrived on site to see how the build was going, there was a large upper-floor support column built in the middle of the main gangway. I had forgotten to rub it out on my work drawings, so it had been built. When my Managing Director turned up, he wasn't very happy about this and told me so in some very choice words.

When I was designing the stand, the MD asked me to make the staircase to his sizes, as after the show he wanted this to be taken out with care for he wanted it for his new house. Also, as I lived in London (the exhibition was in Earls Court), he wanted me to see the pull out to make sure that the staircase would not be damaged, so off I went to the pull out. When I arrived, the head sales rep came over, gave me £5, and said it was for the workmen to have a drink as upstairs. There was a pin and half of Bass bitter (that's about 7 gallon) and a lot of empty ones, so he asked if they could get them all down, empty the ones with beer in them, ready for the brewery chaps to collect in about an hour's time, and off he went. I told the foreman what was required, and his answer was, "You keep the money; we will empty the barrels, no problem."

You can guess what happened. Unfortunately, the staircase got a bit damaged again. I wasn't popular with the MD.

About a year and half later, the company accountant told me that a company were looking for an exhibition designer with a good knowledge of the trade. They had just restarted trading after having a bad time, and this was an avenue they wanted to explore. Also, they were based in Barnet, not so far for me to travel from London, so I was interested.

I had a good think about this and thought I would see if I could get an interview to see what's in the offering. So I rang and got an evening interview. I was shown in a room with four of their staff the MD, his partner, and the art director, and the MD's wife was there to take notes. At first it was quite frightening, but I just sat down and waited for the questions to start. The questions were the normal type – asking about my history, the type of stands I designed, and what wages I was receiving. Then they looked at some of my work. They explained about the company: they had gone through a bad time and were starting a new company to develop modular display units to be used at exhibitions, company shows, shops, and so on. They asked if I would be interested in designing and developing modular displays for this use. I would have to go to see clients, oversee build ups on site, and possibly work weekends as the company's senior designer, with the same wage I was getting, to be reviewed six months later. I asked if I could let them know the following day, and they accepted. Working some weekends would be no problem, as I already do some. I really could do with some extra wages, but I would be saving a few bob on petrol. Being their senior designer sounded good, so I rang them up, accepted, and said I could start in a months' time, after I had given my notice with the exhibition stand contractors.

A month later, I started with the new company and settled in quickly. I found the task in hand challenging and rewarding. Meeting clients, taking briefs, designing, following the jobs up in shops, and helping to developing new modular parts was very enjoyable, but the exhibition was another thing. The unions did not like clients putting up their own stands, but there were ways round this. I already had a sign and display union card, so I could put up some displays providing that

I was doing lettering or work on any of the panels. Another way was the client to have a shell scheme and then put up your own equipment, but this was dodgy. The best way was the client to hire an exhibition stand contractor to put the equipment up for them, but all these things were hassles. I didn't really want to but had to accept it, and many times I had run-ins with the unions. But I was quite happy, as I got my pay rise and had my first bank account.

Then came the bombshell: the lovely old couple who lived above us in our flat moved to an old folks' house in Hemel Hempstead, in the country. This was great news for them but bad for us. We received an eviction notice, so I went to the council for a council house and was told I hadn't lived in London long enough. In reply, I said I was a cockney and lived in London all my life (twenty-six years). Still I got nowhere, so the next thing was to go and see my bank manager in my new bank to borrow some money to buy a place somewhere. He said I could but would have to pay the bank back within three years, so the best thing to do was to put a deposit on a place and take out a mortgage. The bank would lend me £300 to be paid back over three years.

I started to look around for a place, but the property in London was far too costly. I told the design director in the company I was working for, and he and said he would look in the local paper to see if there was anything that might be in my price range. He lived just outside Barnet. He found a little house in Aley Green, near Luton, Bedfordshire. It was about 26 miles from Barnet, but it was a good price: £2600. I offered £2300 and got it for £2400 with a 95 per cent mortgage; the bank paid the 5 per cent deposit as well as the solicitor's fees. So now we lived in the country. It was great for the kids to be out of London. Mind you, the travelling was very tiring and expensive, so I went back to part-time bar work to make some extra cash.

While we were living at Aley Green, I had a bit of a panic one day, when I was working away in my studio and got a phone call from my wife, telling me that Terrie had been whacked with a cricket bat round the face, knocked out, and rushed to the Luton and Dunstable hospital. (I knew Terrie was a bit of a tomboy but what the hell was she doing playing cricket?) Right away, I was on the motorway, headlights on full, speed of the clock, non-stop till I got to the hospital. Terrie was still out, and her face was all one-sided. After about an hour, the doctor told us she would be OK; she had come round, and her face would go back to its shape in a day or so. I can tell you I don't want to go through anything like that again.

Things seemed to be going on well, then along came our fourth child, little Susie. Soon after, my car started giving problems because of the miles I was travelling, so we needed a new car. Money was getting tight, and I was having trouble with my mortgage. I thought that if I could sell, make a bit of a profit, and buy a house nearer Barnet, it would solve all my problems, so this is what I did. I sold the house in Aley Green for £5600 and bought one in London Colney (8 miles from Barnet) for £8200. I was now back on the straight and narrow.

The company's modular systems were really going well, and I was doing a lot more work. With working more weekends, I was getting a better wage. I had my own little studio. It was like a one-man band being paid by a company, for I went and saw the client (which a rep would pass onto me), take a brief, do a design, get the cost, take it to the client for their OK or any alterations, come back and do the work drawings, and see it installed on site. This type of operation was to help me later on, when I went freelance.

Terrie and I were big supporters to the St Albans football club; in fact, I was a VP and we used to go on the players' coach. For recreation, I organised the great pram race in London Colney to raise money for charity. It was for the OAPs in London Colney, and it went towards paying for their Christmas parties, summer outings, and visits.

I was sitting with some lads in a pub, trying to think of an idea to raise some more money for charity. We had already had a couple of tug-o-wars over the little river Colney, which we dammed to make it deeper for the competition, but this was getting played out. One of the lads who had moved down from Scotland told us that in his home village they had a pram race every year, running round the village and having a pint in each of the five pubs.

We all thought it was a great idea, but we had six pubs and two clubs in our village, and to visit them all would be a lot of beer for folks to take on. Also there may be ladies entered. So we reckoned that a half a pint would be more acceptable. Now we had to speak to the pub and club owners to see if they would supply the beer free, as it was for charity. I knew that once one said yes, the others would agree, as they would want to keep their good name in the village. So they all agreed, and we had to work out the route. It would start at a club in the middle, then the next club, onto the most northern pub, and so on, to the river Colney, which would be well dammed and deep, through the river to the last pub. The winners get a trophy. There would be a jazz band in the car park and grub for all. Also, while we were taking part, my kids and some of their mates would have sealed collection boxes and go round the crowd collecting. The route was about 2 miles.

That was it. We were all ready for the great day and praying for good weather and crowds and plenty of entrants. I had done a large poster, had them printed off at work, and had them up all over Hertfordshire. The day was set for August bank holiday.

At last the day came. It was a bright sunny morning with a good forecast for the rest of the day. It was due to start at 11 a.m. I arrived at the start about 10.30, and what a turnout! The village was packed with folks. We had twenty-six entrants, some just dressed up with prams, others with floats built round pram frames. Mine was based on a Wells Fargo stage coach. Me and my friend Alex were dressed as cowboys.

A starter gun was fired, and we all had our first half. Then off we went to lots of cheers. This went on through the whole run. Then we came to the river – by this time it was just over waist deep – and in we went, to splashes from those who were already in and pelted with flour bombs dispatched from the folks watching on the bridge over the river. Finally we went up to the last pub for the last half (but I must say that half was followed by quite a few more), round the back of the pub quick, towel off, changed, then had some grub and a dance to the jazz band.

The following year was even better – the same route, good weather, plenty of folk, and the prams were all floats. The word had gotten round and we had over thirty entrants. I made Stephenson's Rocket to scale, out of a 45-gallon oil drum with a high chimney. I got hold of some smoke-type bombs that the council used to test drains. So with a little water in the drum, the effect was great, and when we went through the river, there was smoke everywhere.

For the third race, I had a lock-up garage round the corner from where I lived, so I started to build a Viking ship in two halves, to be bolted together on the day – complete with sail and all. It took me hours and hours of my spare evening time, but when it was finished, it looked great. Now we were having a very dry summer, and the river was very low. We felt even if we dammed it there still wouldn't be much water, but one of my mates noticed that there was a fire main hose connector pipe stand quite near. So the night before, we went down, dammed the river as usual, but fitted a short fire hose that one of the lads borrowed from his firm and turned it on. Then we took it in turns all night to keep an eye on it. We now had a great head of water, so the hose was quickly disconnected and taken away. The water was chest high. It was nice for the water board to support our charity.

The day had now arrived, the sun was shining again – somebody up there loves us – the kids in their fancy dress were out collecting, and all was set. I had to get another couple of mates to help push this great big Viking ship, so I had one pushing, one inside, and two pulling on ropes. We were all in Viking outfits, three with false beards, one with his own, and all with Viking horned hats (I still have mine). So off we went down our little road to get onto the main Colney road to the start park. As we turned out onto the main road, there were great roars and clapping, for this ship was a well-built 18-foot replica in full colour, complete with full yellow-and-blue sail. The turnout was fantastic, and the floats were magnificent. It was so rewarding to see so much effort put in by the entrants. The many, many spectators clapped and roared as the race started. Now we come to the river, as in the past years the folks on the bridge were all armed with flour bombs. Also, they were waiting for Terrie's great Viking ship to sink in the very deep water. I think some of the other race runners were waiting to see the ship sink too. But old Tel wasn't just a designer for nothing. The inside of the ship was several inflated tractor-tyre inner tubes. No one knew about this but the ship crew. When she was run down the ramp into the deep water, her front came up, and she floated right across the river and up the other side. The only damage was a broken sail mast and lots of flour splatters. It had been a great day again, and it made lots of money for the old folks.

I'm sad to say this was the last one. The Colney committee had a lot of internal political disagreements, and I refused to run it anymore owing to this. But this all happened about six months after, when I approached them to start getting ready for the fourth race.

At work things seemed to change. Whether I was getting more experienced or more confident, I don't know. I was progressing in my job, getting very good at it. Clients and the staff in the company looked up to me. I'd done a lot of redesigning floors in large stores – London, Plymouth, Torquay, Bradford, and many, many, more in large cities, and I loved it. I'd also done quite a lot of exhibitions for different products, but one I was very, very strong in was the toy trade exhibitions.

Then I was told that the MD had sold out to a big organisation. I still carried on doing my own work as I had done for quite a few years, but then one of the directors said I was to be moved into the big studio under a new studio manager the new owners had just hired. I wasn't too happy about this, but I went along with it to see how it would work out. I still had my own clients and carried on as before, but I clashed a few times with the new manager. It came to a head when I had been working for about two days to quite late at night on a big account that was urgent. On the afternoon of the third day, I was putting the finishing touches to their presentation when the new manager told me to stop and go into the showroom to talk to a client. I told him that I must finish what I was doing, but he said, "No – now."

I answered, "Sorry, but I must finish. Get one of the other designers who isn't so busy."

He did. Then about half an hour later, I was called into the office of one of the MDs and was told I had to do what this new manager told me without question. I said, "Sorry, no. I have been with the company for eight and a half years and helped them to get to where they are today; the new manager has only been with the company for three weeks. The MD said I still had to do as I was told, so put in a months' notice. The following day, the MD sent for me and asked me to clear out all my equipment by lunchtime then go to see him. I did so, and he gave me six weeks' money and asked a couple of chaps to see me off the premises. After eight and a half years of my life and devotion to the company I loved, I was out.

On getting in my car I just couldn't drive, as I was crying so much. I just sat there for a while thinking and weeping. Yes, I have had bad days, but it was so very hard to take – after all those years, just chucked out. I found out about a year later from one of the staff that a week after I went, they got rid of the studio manager. Was it a setup to get rid of me? I will never know.

What a fool I was, losing my rag and giving in my notice with four kids, wife, and mortgage to pay and look after. It was no good sitting about feeling sorry for myself. I had to find work or I going to have a lot of money problems. Out I went and bought a local paper for the vacant job pages to see if there was anything I could do. What a shock I had when a vacancy was advertised for a display designer in Watford – somebody up there loves me. I rang the company straight away. The job was still vacant, and when I told them my name, they knew me and said I could go over straight away. On arriving I was met by the MD, who offered me the job without even looking at my work file and photos at the same money I was getting, plus a company car. I could start on the following Monday.

So Monday I got a bus to Watford, as I was getting a car. It was a nice little car, a triumph herald. Again well pleased, I had a chat with some of the staff, who gave me a lot of time and respect. They told me how they had heard of the great work I had been doing for the firm in Barnet and how I got them back on the map, and they hoped I would be able to do the same for them.

I started off by doing a small display design, following it through by sign writings and fixing/mounting the client photos, I was then given half a dozen addresses of companies to make appointments for, to see them to discuss their requirements, then submit designs, as I had been doing with the other company. Everything seemed to be going quite well until I went into my bank at Barnet to draw out some cash for me and to give my wife her household money. The bank teller said that the manager would like to see me. I waited about twenty minutes then went in to see him, and what a shock! He told me that my first cheque from the new company had bounced. I thanked him and said I would go back to the MD and find out what the hell was going on.

I drove straight back to Watford in a very worried and bad mood. Luckily the MD was in. I stormed into his office and demanded what was going on, as my first months' wage cheque had bounced. He said he was so sorry, but they were having problems. That's why they advertised for a new designer, hoping that the new designer would help. Then when I applied for the job, knowing how I had helped the Barnet company to get back on the road to recovery, they thought their prayers had been answered, but it was too late, as the receivers had come in last week and frozen their assets. That was why my cheque had not been honoured, but he said he would give me a personal cheque for five weeks' work. I thanked him for this, and he gave me the cheque. I gave him the car keys, we shook hands, and off I went to get a bus home, the only saviour was that I still had my own car. So now I was out of work again.

After a lot of thought, I decided to try to have a go on my own; all the family were behind me except my father-in-law, who said I was mad and I should get a job. I just ignored him. Drawing equipment, brushes, paint, oil and water, and such, I had. Paper, card, film, vinyl, I had some. It was possibly enough to start with, but I would have to go on the phone, get a garden shed, and turn it into a studio with inside cladding, lighting, heating, and a good drawing board. I knew where there was a good second-hand for sale at a good price, but the main thing I needed was money. I worked it out and reckoned £500 would cover things. So where would I get that type of money? I thought I could possibly ask my dad, but I'm a bloke who wants to do things on his own. So I would go and see the bank manager; he knew what had happened, so I could talk to him, be straight, and tell the truth.

I made an appointment to see him and off I went. I told him what I was going to do, and he sat and listened, saying nothing. After I finished, he just looked at me, then he said, "Right, go out and buy your garden shed. Also get on the phone, but I want two things from you first. You will have to put your house up as a safeguard for the bank; also, I want a report on your progress every two weeks without fail." I thanked him, agreed, and thought he must feel sorry for me.

I bought a shed and fitted it out while I was waiting for the phone to be put on. The shed was right down at the bottom of my garden, so I had to run two hose pipes down to it: one to put the electric cable and the other for the extension phone line, the chap who did the phone was very good, and he didn't charge me for the extra cable used (that's what you can get if you make a good cup of tea).

I was now up and running; all I wanted was some work. So I started to punt about. I got a shop front to sign write, then a sign to do, then a couple of posters, but it was still slow and no money coming in. I sent off my report to the bank, and he was very kind and said, "Don't worry, it will come."

Then one of my mates said, "You have done bar work, haven't you?"

"Yes," I answered, "Why?"

"Well, there is a new manager gone into a Colney pub, and he is looking for bar staff, as the barman who was with the other manager was live-in and has gone with the last manager."

So off I went to see this new manager. I told him my tale and how I used to work behind the bar, and how I used to do all my dad's cellar work.

"OK," he said. "Six evenings a week, no Sunday, behind the bar. Also look after the cellar, and on Sunday mornings, do the pipes." I said OK, as this would give me all day to rep and do any work that I had gotten.

He also asked me if I knew anyone who could do the cleaning as the existing cleaner was retiring. "Yes," I said, "if the cleaner could start a six every morning."

"That would be OK. They could have a key. Who is it?"

"Me," I said.

He laughed and said, "OK, if you think you can handle it."

"No problem," was my reply, "I need the work."

So now I was in the pub trade again, cleaning from six to eight in the morning, home for a shower and a bit of grub, seeing clients and doing work I got during the day, a quick dinner, and I was off working behind the bar starting at seven at night. My young lad, Gary, used to come and help me do the pipes for a couple of bob and a pint of Guinness. He only had one pint as he was still at school. This gave him an appetite for a big breakfast when he got home. My fortnight report to the bank was looking better. Mind you, I did this for nine months, and it nearly killed me, but it made my bank manager a happy chap when I sent him my reports.

My mum and dad had moved down to Devon about a year previous, and as we hadn't had a holiday for a long time, I asked the manager of the pub if I could have a week off. He said OK, so off we went to stay with Mum and Dad, had a good weeks' rest, and was all ready to get back into it on returning.

But on arriving and going down to the pub to let the manager know I was back, I found he no longer was there. A new manager had been appointed, with his own live-in staff. This was a bit of a shock to me as it had been a steady income, but I was doing posters for a Barnet cinema. I used to do the outline drawings, and my daughter used to fill in the colour for me. The sign writing jobs were picking up, as well as doing artwork for a printing company, and the exhibition stand designing was beginning to get better. I was getting a design to do about every three to four weeks, I began to be seen on site again, and my name was getting round as a reliable designer. The organiser of the toy exhibitions was very good; he recommended me to a lot of his exhibitors, so apart from doing his stands, I was doing quite a lot in the toy shows. Large or small stands, I didn't mind. It was all good work; also, I could do all their graphic design. Things were really taking off, so I got planning permission to build a studio on the back of our house, and I came out of the garden shed. The bank manager was a really happy chap now, as I had paid back all my loan.

I was working in the studio on a design, a medium-size stand for a company who made printing machines, and had just finished mounting photos on about thirty panels, all different sizes of coffins and crems, and I was sign writing them. They had to dry off, so I stood them up in the hall and up the stairs in our house (which was not very popular with my wife, I can tell you), when I got a phone call from an old client I'd had when I worked in the Barnet display firm.

I first got involved with this client when he worked for a well-known paper manufacturing company. After I'd known him about a year, he left the paper company and started up as an organiser to do two travelling shows, one for the building trade and the other for the catering trade. They were going to travel all over the British Isles over eight weeks in the large ballrooms of sixteen big four- to five-star hotels. They would leave on early evening Sunday, arrive at the hotel, and set up stands for twelve exhibitors in the building trade through the night, and the show would open at 10 a.m. on Monday. It would finish at 9 p.m. that night, then it would be switched round to the catering trade overnight and open on Tuesday at 10 a.m. Then at 9 p.m. it was finished, it was pulled out and taken to the next city, about 60 to 80 miles away, and the same thing happened. Then when this show was finished off, it went again to another city, but this one was over 100 miles away.

To get this show on the road, he had to have a quick modular panel system that would have an internal electrical system, fascia, and a name tower that would have to go up fast, so he contacted me. We met in a little pub in Barnet for lunch to discuss his requirements. I worked out a rough design on a serviette, and he seemed to like what I had done, so I said that I would do proper drawings then give him a ring. We said our goodbyes, and back to the studio I went with a new challenge.

I drew up my designs of the system based on one of the company's existing modular systems, a typical layout of a show, and some rough costing, then I rang the client and arranged a meeting with him, the design director, and the MD. A week later, we all met in the company's showroom in Barnet. The client liked my designs. Also, he was quite happy with the cost, so an order was placed. But then he asked my MD if it would be possible for me to accompany the travelling show round the country to oversee the build ups and do any extra graphics the exhibitors might require. My MD said yes, but there would be two things: first, the client would have to pay my wages and expenses, and second, would I want to go? The client agreed with the wages and expenses then looked at me. I said I would let him know the following day, as I would have to think about it and speak to my wife.

I spoke to my wife and felt it would be a great experience for me; also, it would be a big chance to get new clients for the future, as there would be a lot of companies exhibiting on this show that I could get work from in the future. My wife just said, "You do what you want to do. You're always working all the time, anyway."

So the following day, I told my MD then rang the client and said it was on. The panels were made, and I had done all the graphic panels that were included in the costing, and it was loaded on three artic lorries – one for shell and the other two for the exhibitors' products – so now the show was on the road.

Obviously there were some teething problems in getting the panels, the client's equipment, and the displays in and out of the hotels' large conference rooms, but it always opened on time. It was a very tiring operation, and you had to grab sleep and food when you could, but I got a lot of new connections, which helped me later by doing displays and exhibition stands when I went freelance. I just thought it would help my company in Barnet.

When the client called, first he asked how things were going and if I was very busy. I told him I wasn't too bad, steady work but not going mad. He then asked me if I would be interested in designing a system for a travelling show similar to the one I'd done for him before: modular, internal electrics, quick to go up, but no poles to fix the panels to, just panels that would strongly lock together, forming a shell scheme, as he had a very good inquiry from a Nordic country to do a travelling fashion show all over the British Isles.

I said yes, of course and said I would give him a ring in about a week with some designs. I finished off the job I was on then and, very excited, started to work out some rough ideas before doing a presentation block plan, elevations, and coloured visual. After about a day, I had worked out a system that would lock together with internal cable for electrics so the panels could be jack plugged together. This would give feed for the clip-on lights I had also designed, then power could be fed in from one end without wires trailing all over the place. I was quite pleased with what I done, so I then started drawing up block plans. About five days later, I rang the client. He said he would call me back once he had set up a meeting with his clients, so we could all meet together. About an hour later, he rang, saying that a meeting had been set for four days' time but he would like me to arrive about an hour early so he could see and run the design that I had done.

Four days later, I went to see him. He was very pleased with what I had done and thought it would work well. The clients were quite impressed and liked it but asked if prototypes of a couple of panels, fixing brackets, and lights could be made. We said OK and we would get in touch when they were ready. They thanked us then left. Then my client said it's now up to you to get the prototypes made also costing for about 100 panels. Also, he said that he would give me the floor plans of the hotels, to work out plans for each show, and he asked me to include in the costings me being on site at every show to supervise the build up and do any other graphics the exhibitors might require. I would have to get back home at the weekend to do any work that had come in. Also, I would have to ring in twice a day, so if anyone had rang with urgent work I could ring them to find out the details. I said OK.

Off I went to a display and exhibition contractor in St Albans. I showed them the drawings and asked if they would make a set of prototype panels for me at cost, and then if the order came, it would be theirs also. I required costing for a 100 panels. They agreed, and I then went and saw a local metal-bracket maker, gave him the drawings, and told him the same as I had told the company who was making the prototypes. He also agreed. Now I had to sort out some form of spotlighting that I may have to modify and design a clip-on arm to hold them. The arm was no problem, but finding a light wasn't so easy. I found one but had to purchase an existing arm that I didn't need; still, you can't win them all.

The prototypes were all now ready, and I had made a mock-up light unit, so an was appointment made, a small room was hired in a London hotel, and the panels were delivered. The clients from the Nordic country arrived at lunchtime. After having a light refreshment, I set up the panels. The clients then had a good look at them and shook and pushed them. My heart was in my mouth. They spoke in their own language to one another then turned, held out their hands, and said, "You have a deal."

It was the first big modular I had designed; there was nothing on the market like it, a panel system that locked together without any poles. I have always said why pay for poles when you don't need them. I was chuffed to bits.

So into production we went with the panels, brackets, lights, and connecting jump leads. Trailing leads to link the panels to power supply plus several wire ramps were also required. The ballroom plans were given to me for the different hotels so I could work out the layouts of each show. It would be six weeks, twelve two-day shows over south England and Wales, then a two-week break and another six weeks in north England and Scotland, starting in Glasgow. On the break, the panels and equipment were stored in a bank of lock-up garages I hired for them in London Conley.

Finally the day came for everything to be loaded on the lorries, and we were off to the first venue. It was the same as the other shows, setting up all night, but the difference with these shows there was a large buffet with Nordic food and drink. This was great, for on the last day of each show what was left was for the chaps who worked on putting the stands up, so once the stand and equipment was loaded and ready to roll the chaps could have a good feed and drink before they were off to the next venue. But because they were exhibition lads, who liked a drink and their grub, there was a problem. On the build ups, working through all night, there was no pop because the bars in the ballrooms in were closed and had large mesh grills pulled down and locked – lots of booze on show but no way of getting a drink. So to me they came and said, "You're the designer in charge; can you get the bar open?" I knew there was no way I could get this done, so wanting to keep the chaps happy, I started to think.

The following day I went shopping. First, I went to a sports shop and bought a very cheap cricket bag. Next, off to a store that stocked centurial heating equipment, where I bought several length of copper pipe, compression joints, and a couple of elbow joints, and I asked in the store if they knew a local firm that could do a little bit of braising welding. What a bit of luck – there was a little firm about 100 yards down the road that repaired damaged cars, so off I went to see them. They must have thought that I was mad, as I asked them if they could braise or weld a little ring on each of the elbow joints. They did it straight away for a couple of quid. Now my last stop was a supermarket to get a pack of cotton wool and a pack of small plastic cups. I was now all set for the next long night shift with the lads, hoping that what I had in mind would work.

The lads were setting up the stands and displays, and I was over at the bar looking at the grill. I got out my metal tape, poked it through the grill to get the distance from the spirit optics to the grill, and once I found that out I called over the manager who was in charge of the workers and asked him if he would help me in getting a drink. He looked very puzzled but said OK. Then I started to put the pipe together, clipping it with the compression joints, then on the end fitted the elbow and placed some cotton wool in the little ring that I had braised onto the elbow. This would absorb any tell tale drips from the optics, then I threaded the pipe through on an angle to the whisky optic, with the elbow under the optic asking the manager to hold a plastic cup under the pipe at the other end. Gently, I pushed down on the pipe, and – presto! – the optic went up and the whisky run down the pipe into the cup. I pulled the tube back out to see if there was any drips, but no, my naughty little invention had worked, and I was a very popular chap with the workers.

Everybody on the build up was happy, and the shows went well. I was glad that the first tour was over, as I had quite a bit of work to catch up with. I wanted to do designs and artwork, so this was going to be seven days a week to get a good name and build up my little company. To get a good name you have to be good, be reliable, and get a good price to get the stands built, but there was a bit of a problem. My wife, who was being influenced by her father, was giving me a bit of a hard time. She and her father just didn't understand the exhibition trade or the world I was living in, and I was getting no help from any of them. Luckily, my daughter understood what I was up against, so she helped me do the bookwork, but writing all the letters, invoices, and such by hand took up a lot of time.

About ten days after the finish of the first tour, my client rang to ask me to a meeting with the Nordic clients so we could talk about the next tour. The meeting was in a small conference room, I was OK as I already had met the Nordic client and they were on every show, but they bought the crown prince of their country with them – bloody hell! But he was OK. He turned out to be a really nice chap, and as the meeting ended he looked at me and said, "You're a Londoner. I think cockney is what you're called. I would like to have a cockney lunch. Which is not a tourist place?"

I looked at him straight in the eyes and said, "I know just where to take you all, a pie 'n' mash shop."

"That's good," was his reply.

In the lift going down from the meeting room my client said, "You can't take the crown prince to a place like that."

My answer was, "Why not? It's good grub, it's clean, also, it's not a tourist visit, and the crown prince wants to see how us real Londoners feed and live. Also, I know he will love it, but if he don't he won't say anything, for he's too much a very nice chap and a gentleman."

We all got in our different cars – me, my client, and the crown prince with two other chaps and two ladies (both these ladies were quite tasty young girls). I led the way to Islington. We found places to park in a side road and walked about 100 yards to a large street market. The crown prince, the two chaps, and the ladies thought it was great to be in a big east end London market and took a lot of photos. Everything was going well so far. Halfway down the market, we came to the pie 'n' mash shop; again, they were most intrigued at the shop, also seeing the live eels on the open side of the shop in a tank. I went in first and saw the manager, told him who I had outside, and said I would pay for all after they had eaten. That was OK by him, so out I went to bring them all in. I said if they liked eels to have eels mash and liquor first, then have pie 'n' mash with liquor after. They asked what liquor was, so I explained.

"OK," they all said. "We will be advised by you."

So up to the counter I went and got the eels mash and liquor and some for myself. I then explained that to get the best taste from the meal, it needed a good shake of pepper as well as the chili vinegar. They listened then applied and started to eat. I could see by their faces that they were enjoying the eels. After they had finished, the crown prince asked if they had any beer or wine. I told him that this type of place didn't have a licence for alcohol. He then asked if it would be OK to drink it if one of his party went and got some.

I went and asked the manager. He said, "I don't see why not, as it is a special occasion." I told the prince it would be OK, so he sent the two chaps out to get some drinks. They were soon back with beer and a couple of bottles of wine, but now there was a problem – no glasses. All the manager had was some big mugs for tea. The prince laughed and said, "OK, they will do." So drinks were poured into the mugs and we all had some, including the shop staff. Then it was the second stage, pie 'n' mash with liquor, pepper, and chilli vinegar, and up I went again to the counter and got the pies. Another winner – they all loved it. After we all had finished eating and drinking, I went over to pay the manager, and he asked me if they would like to be shown round the kitchens. I asked them, and they all said they would love to, so off we all went on a guided tour that was very interesting to all of us.

We all thanked the manager and staff for a wonderful lunch. The crown prince then gave the manager £20 for him and his staff and personally thanked them for a nice time.

The manager cheekily said, "Come again," but the crown prince came back at him and said, "I will, but you get the beers in." Then there were howls of laughter from all. We then made our way back to the cars. The prince and his staff thanked me for a good time and said they would see me on the tour and off they went. I said to my client, "Well?" He said he was wrong to worry, as they enjoyed themselves. "Good," I said, "I will send you the bill for the meal when I get home."

I had caught up with the work that had come in, sent off the designs and costing, and was well pleased to get about 75 per cent of the stands I had designed and quoted for. So when the tour was finished I would have more work, plus several new contacts to do stands in the toy fairs.

Off we went for the next Nordic fashion show. The artic lorries turned up at London Conley and were loaded with all the panels and displays, and off they went to Glasgow. After the lads all went, I said to the manager, "Come home for a drink." He said OK, and God, how pleased we were that he had said OK, for when we got to my house all the lager and snaps for the first show had been delivered to my house and there was a lot.

"How the hell are we going to get it to Scotland?" I looked at the manager and he looked at me.

He said, "There is only one thing we can do; we will have to take it." He had a big Ford and I had a big Jag, so we took our back seats out and loaded all the drinks on our back seats and in our boots. We also had cases on our front seats. The cars were lying very low. We pulled out later that day, and I followed the manager on the drive to Scotland. I saw sparks sometimes from his car as it touched bottom on bumps, and I heard mine do the same, but we got there.

The Scottish shows went well, but we nearly got lumbered with the pipe drink supply, for the bar grill in one of the hotels was alarmed. So as soon as it was touched, a bell went off in the night porter's office.

Lucy, our lookout, spotted him coming and warned us, so quickly put the pipe on the floor, covered it with a panel and stood another panel against the grill. When the porter came to check, he saw the panel up against the grill and told us that it had set his alarm off. He asked us to take it off and make sure we didn't put anything up against the grill again. I said OK and sorry for worrying him. He then left, but we had a dry night.

Back into England, we came to Harrogate; now this was a different type of show. There was a fashion show in the exhibition halls, where our exhibitors had a block of small stands which I had designed, but the main part of their show, with the modular panels and the drinks and buffet, was in the Valley Gardens Sun Pavilion, about half a mile away, so customers had to be transported back and forth. This was done by six large hired taxis with large wooden symbol cut-outs fixed to roof racks. You couldn't miss them, and they looked quite good. Everyone seemed to enjoy what was happening.

On the last day of the exhibition, the crown prince came up to see and was very pleased. He was booked in at the same hotel that me, the manager, and his staff were, so after dinner we all met in the bar. At about midnight, everyone went to bed except the prince, the manager, and me. We wanted to have a few more drinks. As the bar was shut, we had to get them off the night porter, and the prince insisted that he have drinks with us (he didn't need much persuading). He kept on saying he had get any shoes left outside of the rooms to clean, but at about 3.30 a.m., he fell asleep. We just carried on drinking, writing down what we were having so we could pay later. We didn't want to get the porter into trouble for not cleaning the shoes, so we went up to the floors and collected them; there were ten pairs. Finding the cleaning material, we all sat on the floor and polished them, but when we had finished we couldn't remember what room or floors they came from. At 7 a.m., we started to ring rooms where we thought they came from. I can tell you this wasn't very popular, but we did sort it out eventually. Again the crown prince was amused; he was a smashing chap.

We finished the tour and back home I came to find quite a lot of enquiries for stands, graphics, and such and a bit of aggro from my wife.

I started to get on with sorting out the enquiries. I was also thinking of getting a bigger house. The kids were getting bigger and needed more room, and a bigger and better house would help things with me and my wife, I hoped. So we started looking around. We found a nice house in Sandridge, near St. Albans, so we sold the house in London Conley and moved to Sandridge. I bought a very large shed, put it up with a bit of help from a friend, lined it all out, put in shelves, heating, lighting, also the phone, but things were still not right at home.

The kids were growing up fast. I was still working hard, so for a bit of relaxation I joined the Freemasons. Another small tour came and went, and I was now getting involved in some quite nice stands to design and a lot more graphic work (which was handy when the exhibition shows were quiet).

Then came a big shock – I had a phone call from the hospital that my lovely Terrie had overdosed. I rushed to the hospital, went up to the intensive care ward, and saw the sister. She said, "It's OK, don't worry. Terrie will be OK."

I thanked her and noticed that her belt had the Masonic badge on it. I told her I was a Mason, and the sister said that she used to be at the royal Masonic hospital in London, so we had quite a little chat. Then I had another big shock (hadn't I had enough for one day?). The sister asked me if I knew that Terrie was pregnant. I didn't answer, for the sister knew by my face that I didn't.

After a day Terrie came home, I didn't rear up or have a go. I just said there were three ways for her to go: (1) have an abortion, (2) have the baby and never see him again, or (3) get married and find somewhere to live. Terrie, as I thought she would, said they would get married and find a flat.

I said OK, if that's what she wanted, but I would not be going to the wedding. I told her I thought it was a bad choice, for the lad was a bit of a layabout. She got married, and her mum and sisters went. Me and my son Gary didn't go. I sat in the garden and drunk too much then went to bed.

What with me working away on supervising the building of my designs in the exhibition halls and working late, writing invoices, chasing collections for monies owed, I just didn't want the indoor pressure of my marriage. I was beginning to think of trying to get a little flat somewhere, but I was busy with doing designs for the next year's toy fairs. Apart from the organiser's reception, I had another five stands to do; I really didn't have time to look around for a flat.

But then I got a phone call.

I was working away, finishing off the last design I had to do in the toy fair, when the phone rang and someone asked, "Is that Mr Parker?"

"Yes," I said.

"Good. I'm Rosemary, the secretary to Margaret Ensbury of the design council. Ms Ensbury would like to see you in connection with designing shell stands for the design council members in the spring fair at the NEC in February; the organiser of the toy fair has recommended you. When could you come and see her?"

I made an appointment for a couple of days' time, and the secretary said, "That's fine, and I will see you then. When you arrive, ask for her. Goodbye."

I was gobsmacked. Going to do designs for the design council, what a feather in my cap! I went indoors to have a drink on that. My wife asked me why I was so happy, so I told, and all she said was "Oh, really."

Two days later I arrived in the London Haymarket, where the design council's office was, found a multi-storey car park, and parked up on the fourth floor, facing the inside wall. I just sat there for twenty minutes, as I was well early. I leant over to the passenger seat, got my book of pictures of designs I had previously done, and tried to think what I was going to say. To be called into the design council was just unreal. I got out of the car, went down in the lift, and out into the Haymarket. I would've loved to go in a pub that I passed for a drink to steady my nerves, but I was frightened that if I did, I would've wanted to have a wee when having the interview, so I didn't. nervously went in to the council and asked the very posh lady behind the counter, "Please would you let Rosemary, Mrs Ensbury's secretary, know that I am here."

The posh lady said in a posh voice, "It's Ms Ensbury not Mrs."

"Sorry," I said. The posh lady smiled, asked me to take a seat, and picked up the phone.

A few minutes later, a charming young big-breasted lady came and said, "Mr Parker?"

I nodded and said yes, and the young lady asked me to follow her. We went in the lift, and as she went to the operating button, I asked what "Ms" meant. She smiled and said it's a lady on her own, and Margaret was a widow. I apologised for asking, but Rosemary said, "That's OK," and the lift doors opened. Rosemary then led me out to a big open-plan office. I followed her down the middle gangway of the office, and halfway down, met a little short-haired blonde cuddle lady dressed in a three-quarter-length denim skirt, light-brown boots, and a dark, frilly blouse.

Rosemary said, "Margaret, this is Mr Parker."

Margaret put out her hand and said, "Please call me Margaret. Can I call you Terry?"

I looked her in the eyes and said yes, and at this moment, I fell in love with her, just looking at her. I followed Margaret back to her office, wondering what the hell was happening to me. I just wanted to hold her, cuddle her, kiss her – this was mad! You read about this fairy books; it doesn't happen in real life… but it was happening to me.

Margaret then asked me to sit down. She looked at me and asked if I was alright. "Yes," I said, "just a little warm." I don't know how I didn't just say "I love you."

I had to get myself together. It was awful, but I managed to ask if Margaret would like to see some of the designs I had done.

"Please," she answered, so I got my book out of the briefcase, opened it, and passed it book across the desk. As Margaret looked at the photos, I was half looking at them and explaining them to her and half looking at her. After looking at the designs, Margaret looked up from the book and said, "They are very good."

I looked at her – God I just wanted to kiss her, but I had to control myself. Then Margaret spoke again, "I like the modular panel system you have designed, so with a few mods, can you design up something for me to show my bosses?"

"Yes," I very weakly replied. I was sure that Margaret had sensed something in my voice, but she didn't say anything. "Have you a floor plan of the space you have booked?"

Margaret then gave me a small folder with a copy of the floor plan, number and names of the exhibiting members, and some notes of her requirements. Good job Margaret had made some notes, as I was useless. All I could think of was her. I thanked this lovely lady and said I would give her a ring in two or three days to make an appointment to come and see her with my designs.

"That would be great," Margaret answered. She gave me her phone number and said it was lovely to meet me, walked me to the lift. As the lift doors opened and I was going in, Margaret shook my hand, kissed me on the cheek, and said she would wait to hear from me.

I walked out of the lift said goodbye to the posh lady on reception and went to the car park to get my car. Still very confused, I opened the car, got in, put my case on the seat and went to put the key in to start the car. As I did, I looked at the wall in front of me and saw Margaret's face. I just sat there and looked and looked. I couldn't get this lady out of my mind. What the hell was I going to do?

After about ten minutes, I drove down to the barrier, paid, and drove very steadily home. I put the car in the garage, went indoors, and asked if there had been any phone calls. The answer was "I don't know, I was out," so I went out into my studio shed, sat down, and looked at my drawing board, and there was Margaret again. I got my pad out and started to draw her from memory and while I was doing it, I thought of how much I loved her and decided I must hurry and do the designs so I can go and see this lovely lady again. I would kiss her on the cheek this time. God, I so wished it could be on the lips.

I got the designs done very quickly, working late in the night for I knew that as soon as they were finished, I could get to see Margaret again. In two days they were done. I rang Margaret to tell her, and she seemed to be pleased that I had done them so quickly. I made an appointment to see her the following day. I got there about an hour early, but this time I went into a pub and had a large gin and ice to give me some strength and kill a bit of time.

In I went to the design council, saw the posh lady at the reception, and this time I asked to see *Ms* Margaret Ensbury. The posh lady gave me a smile and asked me to take a seat then went on the phone. I sat watching the lift. It seemed like hours, but then the doors opened and out came Rosemary.

We went up in the lift, and Rosemary showed me into Margaret's office and said, "Margaret won't be long, as she is just finishing off a meeting with her director. Also, Margaret knows you're here."

After about five minutes, Margaret came in and said she was so sorry to keep me waiting. I didn't care, Margaret was there. I stood up, shook her hand, and gave her a kiss on the cheek. If only Margaret had known how long I had waited to do that. She looked lovely as usual in a brown fitted trouser suit. The top was in the style of an army battle dress and went just down to the waist. The trousers were quite tight, showing a nice little bootie, and her blouse was a very light tan. Margaret then went round her desk and sat down. I still stood, taking the designs out of my case then laying them on the desk in front of her. I walked round her desk so I was at her side to explain the fine details. God, she smelt good. We chatted for about half an hour. Then Margaret said, "It seems just what the members require," but it will have to be OK'd by her bosses, and she asked about the price.

I told her, "I will have a price by midday the following day, as I have asked a smaller little company to give me a cost. I think the bigger firms would be a bit heavy when they knew it was for the design council."

Margaret laughed, said I was right, and thanked me for thinking of that. We had another little chat then we walked off to the lift. Margaret said she would await my call with the price tomorrow, gave me a kiss on the cheek, and said goodbye. I got in the lift, so sad to leave her. I came out of the offices wishing I was just going in, but I didn't forget to say goodbye to the posh lady on the way out. I thought about Margaret on the drive all the way back.

When I got home, I went into my studio, rang the contractor, and told him that I was a third of the way there. He said he would ring me through with a price that evening. "OK," I said, "That's good."

About 9 p.m., he rang me through with the price. It seemed a fair price. Now had to work out my costs for the designs, visits to the council's offices – although I would do these for nothing just to see Margaret – and being on site at the NEC Birmingham. I rang Margaret the following morning and gave her the price. She said I was in budget, but the designs were still with her bosses, so once we finished talking, she would go up and give them the cost and hopefully be able to ring me later that day.

That afternoon I was on the drawing board trying to do some artwork, but my mind was only on one thing, Margaret. I came out of my studio, went into the lounge, and poured myself a very large gin and ice. My wife spotted me and said, "What's the matter with you? These last few days, you're walking about as if you're in a dream, and now you're boozing. I'm getting fed up with you – you should have never worked for yourself." Then she slammed the door and went out, I didn't have the chance to say anything, so I drank my gin and ice then poured another and went back into the studio.

I sat there drinking the gin and wondering what the hell I was going to do about my marriage, which had been drifting away for over a year. What was I going to do and tell my kids? What about Margaret, the wonderful lady who I fell hopelessly in love with – she didn't know, and how and when would I tell her? What would happen then? God, what a mess. I finished my gin and went into the house to get another. My wife was still out, thank God, as I couldn't handle an argument.

I tried to work out things in my mind. The gin was beginning to kick in, as I had done about half a bottle by now. I started to try to write down things that I might say to Margaret, and the phone rang. I jumped, then quickly thought, *This must be Margaret. Should I tell her now the feelings I have for her? No, no, not on the phone, I have got to tell her face to face.* I picked up the phone took a deep breath and said hello.

"Is that you, Terry?" It was my lovely Margaret. "Are you alright, Terry? You sound a little down."

What a clever lady, to hear the trouble I was having. "Yes," I said, "a little bit tired."

Margaret then said, "You will be pleased to know that my bosses like the designs and the price. Is there any chance of you popping to see me tomorrow?"

"No problem. What time?" I asked.

"About 11 a.m.," Margaret replied.

"That's OK. I will see you then." We said goodbye to one another and hung up. I was over the moon. The gin was now telling me this would be the time to tell this lady I love her. Yes, I decided, that's what I would do, without fail. I turned off the lights and locked my studio and went into the lounge for another gin, which I had. I turned on the TV and sat in the chair.

About an hour later, my wife said, "Your dinner is in the oven, if you want it. We have had ours. Also, you can sleep down here tonight, as I don't want you upstairs."

I just said, "You can please yourself and turn off the dinner, as I don't want any."

She walked out, shutting the door rather loud, and I thought, *Silly cow.* I got up and had another gin. About three in the morning I woke up, freezing cold, and the TV was making a funny noise, so I got up, turned off the telly, got a big old coat from the cupboard in the hall, came back, got into the chair, covered myself up, and went back to sleep. Tomorrow would be a great day, as I would be seeing Margaret again.

I awoke about 7 a.m. and had a mouth like a sewer. I went into the kitchen to make a coffee. The kids were up, flying around, and so was my wife. Nothing was said. I drunk my coffee, had a shower and got dressed, and told my wife I was going the design council in London, if anyone calls, and I should be back about mid-afternoon. She looked at me and said, "Going to see that woman again."

I asked, "What do you mean by that?" I was a bit worried I had let something slip.

"The one you keep talking about as a very nice lady."

I said, "That lady is just a client," but in my heart it was lies. I said goodbye but got no answer. I got the car out of the garage and off I went to see Margaret. Although it seemed a long drive, I got to the Haymarket early, went round the corner to a little café and had a little late breakfast, then left the café and went to the council offices. I walked in, and the posh lady looked at me and smiled and said, "You have come to see Margaret."

"Yes," I said and went and sat down. *The lady is getting to know me now,* I thought, *as it's "to see Margaret", not "Ms Ensbury".*

As I was sitting thinking this, a voice that I had been waiting to hear again said, "Hallo, Terry."

It was Margaret; the lady had come down to fetch me instead of sending Rosemary. My heart thumped. *Has Margaret realised that I love her dearly? I wonder, Or is it just hopeful thinking?*

We went up to her office and both sat down. Margaret asked if I would like a coffee. "Yes, please," I said, and two coffees were ordered. We started to discuss the design and what type of graphic would be required. I started to make some notes and thinking of telling Margaret about my feelings when there was a knock on the door, and in came Rosemary with the coffee. *Good,* I thought, *I will drink the coffee then tell her.*

But there was another knock on the door and in came a tall gent. Margaret stood up and said, "This is my director."

We shook hands and he said, "So you're the famous Terry Parker the toy organiser talks about."

I just said, "I hope the reports are good." He laughed and then we all talked about the modular panel system I had designed for them. He asked if I could arrange for it to be stored for future use after the show, and I said I would look into it for him and let Margaret know (another excuse to speak to Margaret).

"Good," he said. We then shook hands and he left.

I said to Margaret, "He seems like a nice chap."

"He's OK," she replied. We talked a bit more about the layout, then Margaret asked if it would be possible for me to attend if she set up a meeting with all the design council exhibiting members to discuss the build up and any extras that may be required at the show.

"No problem," I said. "Just let me know the time and the place. Also any time you need to talk and discuss anything, let me know and I will come and see you."

Margaret looked at me and said, in a way I just can't describe, "That's a wonderful service you're giving me."

The way it was said made me wonder, *Has Margaret got some feelings for me? I don't know, but I'm sure there was something.*

We went to the lift, and again I got a kiss on the cheek. She said, "Thank you, and I will give you a ring about the meeting with the members ASAP."

We said goodbye and I got in the lift thinking again how I bottled out and didn't tell her my feelings. I'm not such a big strong bloke I thought I was. With this still on my mind, I got out of the lift and walked to the door. I heard a lady's voice say, "Goodbye, Mr Parker." I looked round, and it was the posh lady on the reception.

I said, "I'm sorry, I was miles away."

"That's OK," she said. That was very bad of me, as I always try to be polite to everyone especially nice ladies.

About a week passed, and there were still a lot of problems with things indoors, but what did I expect? My wife didn't understand my work, I was very quiet, and I was in deep love with another lady who didn't know. *What a mess. Things just can't keep going on like this. It's driving me mad; also, I'm drinking far too much. I'm starting about 10 a.m.* This was all going through my mind while I was sign writing a small board for a local garage in my studio when the phone went.

"Hallo, is that you, Terry?" My heart raced. All my worries went. "Are you free next Tuesday?"

"Darling, I'm always free for you," I said without thinking. *What did I say that for? Have I blown it?* Margaret just laughed. *Thank God for that*, I thought.

Margaret went on, "I have arranged for a meeting here at the centre for 10.30 a.m. with the exhibiting members, and I would like you to meet them all to have a chat. There will be refreshments at lunchtime, as it will go on till about 4 p.m."

"No problem, Margaret. I will be there at ten."

I walked into the council offices dead on time. The posh lady smiled and said, "Would you go up to the conference room on the fourth floor? I will ring through and let Rosemary know you're on your way."

On getting out the lift, I was met by Rosemary, who took me into the large conference room. There was Margaret, talking to her director. They both came over and shook my hand and Margaret gave me my usual kiss on the cheek. My day was starting good.

After a while, the exhibiting members started coming in, and soon the room was buzzing. Margaret introduced me the members, who asked about the stand and when I thought they would be able to dress and put up their own point-of-sale displays. I was kept very busy. After the lunch refreshments, the members gradually started to go. The director went after they had all gone, just leaving Rosemary, Margaret, and me.

Margaret said, "Let's sit down for ten minutes, have rest and a cup of coffee." We sat chatting about the way things had gone, and Margaret asked if I was happy with everything.

I said yes. (I would've liked to say, "Can I have a kiss?") About half-hour later, Margaret said, "Well, that's it. We must get on and tidy up the room, and I expect you, Terry, want to get home."

"No," I said, without thinking. It just came out. Margaret looked at me, puzzled. I had never seen her look at me like that before.

"What do you mean?" she asked.

I replied, "Things at home have been going wrong for about a year now."

Margaret then gave me a little comforting smile and said, "I'm so sorry for you. It must be very hard."

I then thanked her, got up, and said goodbye to Rosemary. Margaret then said she would see me to the lift. She gave me my usual kiss, but it seemed different. It seemed harder, or maybe I was just hoping. I was nearly crying. I just wanted to grab and cuddle her, but I said a quick goodbye, saying I would ring her later in the week to let her know how things are going with the making of the equipment. I got out of the lift with my head down, rubbing my eye. The posh lady spotted me and asked if I was OK. "Yes," I said. "Just got something in my eye, but it will go in a minute." I said goodbye and headed back to the car park, got in the car, and cried my heart out. God, how I so wanted to cuddle that lady.

I got home to the usual reception: "Been to see that fancy woman again?" I don't go with men hitting a woman, but I came close. I went out, unlocked my studio, got a bottle of gin out of one of my filing cabinets (yes, I had a supply of gin in my studio now), gave myself a good measure in a glass sat at my drawing board, and started to drink.

After about half an hour, I checked what work was urgent to do – not a lot, thank God, just a little bit of artwork for a local printer. It was just a label to design for a whisky bottle. There was no rush for the other couple of jobs that I had to do. I started to rough it out when the phone rang.

I picked it up, and the voice on the other end said, "Terry?" I trembled; it was Margaret. "I'm just ringing to see that you got home safely, as you seemed a bit distressed when you left, and I was a bit worried."

"Margaret, thank you, it's kind of you to think about me," I answered.

"Are things any better?" Margaret asked.

"No, they are getting worse."

"Don't worry. You will sort it out, I'm sure, and everything will be rosy again."

I thanked her again and said, "I don't think so, as it has gone for such a long time now.

Margaret said she was sorry this was happening to me, and if she could help in any way please give her a phone. We said goodbye and hung up. By now my glass was empty, so I filled it up again and thought about what Margaret had said. If she could help... *If only I could tell her how much I love her, maybe we could cuddle. I have just got to find away to tell her.* I was a bit frightened of losing her, for I didn't know if she had a boyfriend. I knew Margaret went ballroom dancing, and you can't dance on your own. I would have to chat with one of my Mason brothers who is going through a divorce at the moment, to see what he thinks.

The following morning I drove over to his pub. We had a drink, and I told him what was happening. He was the first person I had told. He listened and said, "You have got to tell her otherwise you'll go barmy. You don't know, this Margaret might feel the same about you."

I said, "I wish."

He replied, "You won't know until you make a move." I drank up thanked him and left, still not knowing what to do.

The weeks passed. I was in contact with Margaret every day, finding excuses to go and see her. The build up for the show would not come quick enough; meanwhile, I was doing my other work and still getting problems indoors, also drinking too much, plus a couple of other things – one, I wasn't sleeping, and two, things had been said to my mum and dad.

At last, build up time had come. The panels and displays had been loaded and were on the way. I was on site getting the carpet laid in the morning so the panels could be delivered and start to be erected in the afternoon. The best thing was that Margaret would be there tomorrow.

Things went well; the carpet was down and the panels were being unloaded. The contractor told me that they were going to start erecting in about an hour. *Great,* I thought, *there will be a good show for Margaret when she arrives tomorrow.*

The following day, Margaret arrived with Rosemary. She came over to me, gave me a little hug and her normal kiss on the cheek. Margaret then said, "It's looking good, and you seem to be well on." The sparks had started putting their chaser cables. By that time, it was time to go. Margaret and Rosemary were going to their hotel in Birmingham by train. I walked with them to the station, kissed Margaret on the cheek, and said I would see them tomorrow.

The following day I was on site early but had a big shock; some of the panels had slightly twisted. I asked the contract foreman what he thought had happened. He said, "On the build up the heating is turned off at night, and being February, it gets a bit damp in the halls, but on the last day of the build, also when the show is open, the heating is left on a trickle all night."

When Margaret arrived, I explained, but by then the heating was on and the panels were going back into shape. I also told her that to keep the cost down for them, I had the core of the panels made in slightly softer wood than beech, as beech would have been twice as much.

The stands were starting to take shape and started to look good. Also, some of the exhibitors started to come in. The last day of the build up came, and everything was ready by lunchtime, apart from little bits of odds and ends to be done. Everyone was well pleased.

About 4.30 p.m., I went over to Margaret and asked her if she was doing anything that night, and I said if not, I would like to take her out to dinner.

Margaret looked at me, put her hand on my arm, and said with a grin, "Are you trying to bribe me?"

"No, I often take clients out to lunch or dinner, and you're a special client to me."

"OK," she said, "What time?"

"About 8 p.m. at your hotel," I answered. Again I walked Margaret back to the railway station; Rosemary had already gone with one of the members. I waited for the train to come and gave Margaret a quick peck on the cheek as she got on the train. Then it was back to the hotel to get tarted up to take Margaret out. I was so, so happy.

I got back to the hotel and got a drink to take up to my room. I sipped at the drink then jumped in the shower, dried off, had another sip of my drink, put on my trousers and sorted out a shirt, had another sip of the drink – it was nearly gone now. I made up my mind I wouldn't have any more till I got to Margaret's hotel. I slapped on a bit more aftershave and finished my drink. It was now nearly seven, so I was ready to go. I got to the door then stopped. I needed the name and address of the hotel.

Luckily Margaret had given it to me in case of any problems on site. On the way out, I asked the porter for directions in Birmingham to the hotel. Birmingham is a big place. He looked at a map and said, "Go off at spaghetti junction and follow the signs to the railway station. Opposite the station there is a one-way street on your right. Go down that street to the end; it bears right. Follow the road round, and the hotel is on the right. It should be OK to park along there this time at night."

I thanked him and asked what the name of the one-way street was. He laughed and said, "Station Road." I smiled and thought what a fool I was.

I got in the car. It was now ten past seven, and off I went, thinking, *I hope the directions are right. I don't want to get lost in Birmingham and be late.* It was OK; I found the hotel spot on, and I parked nearly outside the entrance. The time was seven forty-five. I could go in the bar and have a drink, then in about ten minutes, I would go to reception, ring through, and let Margaret know I was in the bar. I went over to the lady on reception and asked her if she would ring Margaret Ensbury's room and tell her that Terry had arrived and was in the bar. Everything was going well so far, but my heart was in overdrive.

I sipped at my drink, looking at the entrance. Then, in Margaret came. She looked a million dollars. I said, "You look lovely." Margaret smiled and thanked me. "Would you like a drink before we eat?"

"Thank you, a gin and tonic would be nice."

So I ordered two gin and tonics, as I had finished my drink. We said cheers to one another then sipped at our drinks.

I then asked, "Where would you like to eat, here in the hotel or out?"

Margaret then asked me if I liked Indian food, as there was a very good little restaurant about five minutes' walk.

"That sounds fine to me," I said. We finished our drinks left the bar and went out into the street. She put her hand on my arm I then put my right hand across and laid it on her hand. We looked at one another and smiled – God, I was so happy.

The little restaurant was very nice and not too busy. I asked, "Shall we have a bottle of wine?"

Margaret said, "That would be nice."

"Medium dry?"

"That will be lovely."

We had a nice meal and chatted about exhibitions and a little about each other. It was very relaxing. After we had finished our meal and wine, I asked Margaret if she would like coffee.

"I would love one," she said. So I ordered two coffees.

I knew I had to say something. I just couldn't go on as it was. I looked at Margaret and said, "I have something I have got to say to you."

She looked at me with a very puzzled look. I took a deep breath – I was really shaking then – finally got the courage, and I said it. "Margaret, I love you and have loved you since we first met."

At first I didn't think Margaret was going to answer, but she did. "Don't be so bloody silly. Push off – you have a family."

"I'm sorry, but I can't help it."

"I think we should go now."

I paid the bill, and we went out in the street. I then offered my arm, but Margaret refused. I said, "I will walk you back to the hotel."

"No, you won't, push off."

"You can't go back on your own."

"Alright, then." We walked back, and not a word was spoken. We got to the hotel, and I said, "I will see you in."

No was the answer, and Margaret went in alone quite upset, but as not as upset as I was. I had upset the lady I loved so much. *What the hell am I going to do now?* I drove back to my hotel, crying all the way and thinking what a fool I was, telling her like that.

I finally got to the hotel and went straight to my room. I didn't even have a drink; I made myself a cup of instant coffee, burnt my lip as I tried to drink it too quick, and sat looking at the wall, again thinking, *What an idiot I have made of myself.* On that, I got undressed and got into bed, but sleep didn't come easy. About 7.30, I decided to ring Margaret at her hotel and try to talk to her. I knew she would be up, as she would leave early to the NEC. It was opening day. I got through to the hotel without any problem and asked if I could be put through to Margaret Ensbury's room. I waited a couple of minutes and Margaret answered. I said, "Hallo, Margaret."

"What do you want?" she answered.

"I'm so sorry," I said, "but I love you dearly."

"Push off." Margaret hung up. I'd mucked it up again, but I just couldn't help it. I was speaking from the heart.

I went down had a little bit of breakfast. I didn't really want any. I checked out and paid the bill then drove to the NEC. I got to the stand about ten, as there was a lot of traffic going in. I went straight to the stand. It was very busy, lots of buyers, Margaret and Rosemary were on the reception talking to the buyers, members, and other design council staff. The whole stand was buzzing, I waited till Margaret was free and I went over to her and said, "We have got to speak before I go back."

"I have nothing to say to you. Also, I haven't got the time because as you can see, the stand is very busy."

"Yes, I can see that, but you must get a lunch break. Surely you can give me five minutes then, please? We are friends."

"Are we?" Margaret answered. I just stood there and looked at her. "Alright," she said, "Give me half an hour. Where will you be?"

"I will be just walking round the stand, looking at the products on show."

In about half an hour, Margaret found me and said she had a twenty-minute break, so we went into one of the other hall's restaurants. I got two coffees and we sat down. Then Margaret said, "Now what's this all about? I have been awake nearly all night thinking about it."

I said, "I'm sorry about that, but I haven't been able to sleep properly since I met you. You see, Margaret, I fell in love with you when I first saw you, and my love for you has been growing for you stronger day after day. I just can't help myself."

Margaret looked me in the eyes, and I could see there was some feeling there. "But you have a family; you can't love me."

"Margaret, I just love and worship you. Please, please, don't tell me to push off."

She looked at me again and said, "Terry, I won't say that again, but now I must get back as my director is coming up this afternoon." I walked back with her to the stand. I said goodbye and I would see her on the pull out and if she had any problems, please give me a ring. I then got hold of her hand and gave her a loving kiss on the cheek twice, then walked away very sad.

I arrived home to the normal welcome, just ignored it, and went into my studio and put a very, very, large gin in a glass and had a good swig. After about half an hour, I went back in the house an asked if there had been any calls.

"Yes," was the answer, "two companies, who left their numbers and another of your fancy women, who said I had her number."

I said, "You're mad – this lady is a very good client to me, and she gives me a lot of work.

"What do you give her in return?"

I thought, *It's no good in saying anything, as she won't believe me,* so I went back into the studio have another drink then answer the clients that rang.

The lady who rang was a good friend, and she wanted to see me about a big project they wanted to do later, up in Scotland. The lady told me that my wife was quite rude to her on the phone.

I said I was sorry and that we'd been having problems for the past year. The lady understood and said she hoped that any other clients would also understand. I said, "So do I," then made an appointment to see her the following week.

After talking to her I started to think about getting a flat again and leaving. After about an hour, I started to work out a design for a stand for a client who was exhibiting in a building exhibition in London. After a while, I stopped and thought about Margaret and got a bit weepy. I had another drink and made up my mind to go to the show tomorrow to see her. I then decided to finish for the day and go in the house and unpack. When I went in, my wife said there were new sleeping arrangements. She had moved all my clothes into Terrie's old room, "so you can sleep there." I just said OK; I was too tired to argue.

The following morning I was up early. I finished off the design I was doing and then locked the studio. I went in the house, had a sandwich, and said, "I'm off out."

"Going to see your fancy woman again?"

I didn't answer but thought, *You are nearly right, but it's not a fancy woman, it's a very lovely lady.*

I decided to go to the NEC by train. I got to the show by mid-afternoon and went straight to the stand. The first one I saw was Rosemary. She said, "Hallo, Terry. I didn't expect to see you today."

I said (telling pokies), "I had a meeting with the firm I use to lay my carpets for me, so I thought I would pop in to see how things are going. Where's Margaret?"

"She has just gone to the press office. She will be back in a minute."

I had a quick walk round the stand and spoke to a couple of the members to ask how things were going. They all seemed happy. Margaret came back and came over to me. As I kissed her on the cheek, she said quietly, "What the hell are you doing here?"

I whispered, "I've come to see you because I love you."

Margaret stepped back and said, "You don't give up, do you?"

"No," was my quick answer. Margaret then gave me half a smile and went back to her little office on the stand. I took a deep breath, had another walk round the stand, had a chat to a couple more of the members, then went to Margaret's little office. "Have you time to have a quick drink with me before I go back, Margaret?"

"Of course she has," said Rosemary. *Has she guessed that I'm in love with her boss or is she just being nice to me?*

Margaret said, "Come on then, just a quick drink, as I have work to do."

I looked at Rosemary and said thanks; she looked at me and said, "That's OK," smiled, and winked. *She must know,* I thought.

We went to the bar and found a seat. Margaret sat down and I went and got two gin and tonics. I came back and sat down, and before Margaret had chance to say anything, I looked her straight in the eyes and said, "I had to see you again, as I love you so much."

Margaret picked up her drink, had a sip, and said, "You're mad."

"Maybe, but that doesn't alter my feelings for you."

"But you don't know anything about me," she said.

"I don't care, Margaret. You're my life."

"And you're silly," she said, "so you have got to get yourself together. Now I must go back to the stand." We both finished our drinks and went back to the stand, I gave her a strong kiss on the check. Margaret gave me a lovely look with her big eyes and said goodbye. I left feeling a lot better than I arrived.

When I got in, I asked, "Any calls?" There was no answer. My wife just gave me a bit of paper with a name on it. I thanked her, went to my studio, and got the gin bottle out again. I looked at the bit of paper. It was the chap I did work for at the little printing firm, so I rang him. He had an urgent job for me, so I said would see him tomorrow.

He had about a six-hour job for me that he needed by the following day. I shot home. I hadn't been in the studio five minutes when the phone rang. It was the client that I'd done the tours for, asking if I could see him later, 11 a.m. tomorrow, as he wanted me to work out and run a office and drawing exhibition in a few months' time. He had left messages, but I hadn't rang back.

I wasn't going to be able to see Margaret till Thursday afternoon on the pull down, so I started working as fast as I could. As I was working, I remembered that I had promised to sign write a fairing on a racing motorbike on Saturday morning. I finished the printer's artwork then started on the panels for Harrogate, knowing I had all day Friday, Saturday afternoon, and Sunday. I was up early Thursday morning and at the printers at 9.30 a.m. I was on the road to London by ten, into the client at eleven. The briefing took longer than I'd thought it would, and I didn't get on the road to Birmingham till 1.45 p.m. I got to the NEC about 3.30 p.m. and rushed to the stand. I looked round. No Margaret. I saw Rosemary and asked, "Where's Margaret? I must see her," then bit my tongue realising what I had said.

Rosemary smiled and said, "I know."

"What do you mean, you know?"

She smiled again. "I'm not silly, and I watch; you think the world of her."

"I know, but does Margaret have any feelings for me?"

"I'm saying nothing," Rosemary answered. "Anyway, Margaret has had to go back to the office, as there is a meeting of top management. It had to be today, as Margaret has a day's leave tomorrow."

I felt sick. Looking at Rosemary, I said, "I know Margaret lives near Olympia Hammersmith; do you know where?"

"Yes, but you know I can't tell you that."

"Rosemary, if you think you know how I feel about Margaret, you would help me. I would never say where I got it from." And here I put my cards on the table. "I fell in love with her the first time we met."

Rosemary smiled and said, "I know you're in love with her, but I didn't know it was as soon as that."

"So if you know that, please give me her address."

She smiled again. "I will give you the road, but not the number, but don't knock on number 35 or 39." Then she told me the street. I gave her a big cuddle and kiss on the cheek. "Good job Margaret's not here, as she would have got jealous." We both laughed. Then I said, "You, young lady who knows all, does Margaret love me?"

The reply was, "Fifth amendment."

I thanked her for giving me some hope, and if it did leak out how I got the address, I told her she could say I had some urgent drawings to give her.

I then went over to the contractor's office asked if they were all OK for the pull out and storing the panels. They said it was no problem. I thanked them and drove home, thinking about how and when I was going to see Margaret again. Friday's out, so was Saturday morning, but the afternoon or evening would be OK. I would ring another Masonic mate who had a van hire company and ask him to give me a ring about seven, asking me to go to a Masonic meeting Saturday evening. I could put on my dark clothes, then find a lay-by on the way and get another coat, which I had already put in the boot, take off my tie, then call on Margaret in casual clothes.

On getting home, I went into my studio and rang my friend and asked him to ring to invite me to a meeting about seven. He asked, "You playing away?"

"No, I will explain to you when I see you."

Again he said, "You're playing away, you dirty little bugger." Again I said no. "OK, have it your way then. I will ring about seven."

I made sure I was in the toilet just before seven so someone else answered the phone. Spot on seven the phone went. My son answered it and said, "It's your friend, Dad."

I came out of the toilet, picked up the phone, and thanked him for his invite. I said to my wife, "I'm going to a Masonic meeting on Saturday."

"You go where you like," was her answer, "as they are all weird blokes running round with their trousers rolled up." This gave the kids a big laugh. Things have been said, and with me sleeping in another room... I wasn't in their eyes the greatest dad in the world.

I worked very hard the following day and managed to sneak out a coat and put it in the boot. I finished about six, had a bit of dinner on my own, as the wife and kids had already eaten, got another gin, and sat back in the chair. I don't know what time I fell asleep, but I was cold when I woke up about in the early hours. I looked at my glass; there was a mouthful left, so I drank that and went to bed. I didn't wake up till nine – sod it, I wanted to start early. So a quick shower and it was out to the garage were the motor bike was to be sign written. The guy said to me, "You're a bit late today."

"Yes," I said, "I overslept."

"OK, well, the bike is over there, and this is what I would like on the fairing."

"OK, no problem."

He then asked, "Have you eaten anything?"

"No," I replied.

"I will get you a roll when I go over the shop to get mine."

"Great," I replied. I started work on the fairing, but it was taking longer than I thought. I finished about three; good thing the bike owner paid me cash.

I rushed home to have a quick shave, got dressed in my dark suit, put a London A to Z map in my Masonic box, shouting, "Don't wait up!"

The answer was, "Don't worry, we won't." I laughed and went out the door. I drove about 5 miles, stopped in a lay-by, and changed. I got the map book out to work out my route, then off I went, thinking, *I'm going to see Margaret again, but what reception will I get?*

It was about six thirty when I found Margaret's street. There was a pub at the bottom of the street, so I thought I would have a quick drink to give me a bit of Dutch courage before I knocked on the door. The pub was long and narrow inside with a few folks in. I asked for a large gin and tonic with ice and sat down, trying to think of what to say. *I could ask her out to have a meal. Yes, that's a good idea. I'm starving, only having a roll this morning.* I was also thinking that it was a good job I'd changed my coat and tie, as I would have looked a bit out of place in this little pub. I had another drink and looked at my watch – nearly seven thirty and dark.

There wasn't a space outside of 37. I remembered Rosemary had said, "Don't knock on 35 or 39." I hoped she wasn't having a joke on me. I opened the little gate to the little front garden. I held my breath. I could hear my heart thumping as I rung the bell. In seconds, the door opened and there was a young short, dark-haired young man. I thought, *Has Rosemary set me up?*

Then I asked, "Does Margaret Ensbury live here?"

"Yes, she's my mum, but she's out dancing."

"Where?" I asked.

"At her dance club."

"What time does Margaret get back?"

"About ten to ten thirty," he said. Then he asked, "Who are you?"

"I'm a friend who worked with her at the design council."

"Ah, OK," he said.

I said I would call later then thanked him.

I sat there in my car for a long while trying to think what to do next. I was so upset that Margaret wasn't in. I drove round the block towards Olympia and spotted a fish and chip shop, got some fish and chips, sat in the car and polished them off I was so hungry. I looked at my watch; it was nearly nine. There was a pub just along from the fish and chip shop. I could go and kill an hour then go back at ten and wait for Margaret to come home. *Then what, knock on the door at that time of night? Yes, I have got to see her.*

At ten to ten, I made my move, after only having two drinks. At her house, the lights were still on downstairs. I was getting cold. Then the lights went on in one of the upstairs rooms and off downstairs. It was ten fifteen. I thought, *Have I cocked it up; has the lad gone to bed early and that's Margaret going to bed?* I was worried. Then a car pulled up. Margaret and an elderly chap got out. *God, what's this? Has Margaret got a boyfriend?* My heart dropped as they both went in. I just sat there crying. *Surely Rosemary would have told – or did she know?*

About twenty minutes later, I was just thinking of going home heartbroken, but the door opened and out came the bloke. I was out of my car and ringing the bell before his car was out of sight. When the door opened, there was lovely Margaret, looking shocked. "What the bloody hell are you doing here?" she said.

"I'm sorry, but I had to see you. Please, may I come in?"

"No, you can't."

"Please."

"No."

"Then please can I come and see you tomorrow afternoon? I have to sort myself out, please, please."

Margaret thought for a moment then smiled and said, "Alright then about three, now you go home, and drive safely."

"Thank you," I said. "Please can I have a kiss?"

"No, you can't. Now go."

"OK. I will see you tomorrow."

Driving home, I thought, *What work have I got to do that can be done on Monday? Only to finish a couple of panels. Also, what excuse can I make to get out Sunday afternoon?* I got on the M1. Then it came to me. *I will say the car is playing up. I will work on it in the morning then take it out to test in the afternoon – sounds good.*

About a mile from my house I stopped, changed, and went home. All the lights were out when I got there, so I crept in and went to bed.

The following morning, I checked how much I had to do on the panels, then I said that I was going in the garage to see if I can find the problem. I got no answer, so I went out and mucked about, taking out the plugs. I came in about twelve thirty and said I was going for a shower and would road test the car after lunch.

It seemed to take hours, but at last I was at Margaret's house. Margaret opened the door and asked me to come in. As I did, I kissed her on the cheek, and Margaret showed me into her front room, and there, sitting on the couch, was her son. Margaret said, "I believe you have already met. Terry, this is Ralph, and Ralph, this is Terry."

He shook my hand and sat down again. "Would you like a cup of coffee?" Margaret asked.

"Please," I replied.

"Ralph?"

"No, Mum. I'm going round to see Fred in a minute."

The coffee came up, and we all just chatted. As I was drinking the coffee, Ralph stood up and said, "I'm off now, Mum. Nice to meet you, Terry," and off he went.

Margaret came and sat next to me and said, "Now what's this all about, Terry?"

"Margaret, I'm so sorry, but I love you so much. I fell in love with you when I first saw you and just can't live without you. I'm thinking of you all the time." By this time, I had tears in my eyes.

She looked at me lovingly, took hold of my hand, and said, "Terry, I also love you dearly and have for a long, long time." I then pulled her to me and kissed and kissed her.

"You have made me the most happiest man in the world." We then just sat together cuddling for a long time.

Then Margaret said, "What about your family?"

I said, "Margaret, you just don't know. Things haven't been right for over a year now. We even have separate rooms. I get no support, apart from my work. I have to do all the invoices, et cetera, but I think of you and I'm OK." We kissed again.

We sat and discussed things. Margaret would tell her three children. I asked if things would be alright. Margaret looked me in the eyes and said, "I don't care if they're not, as I have you by my side. What about you? Do you realise you could lose everything you have worked for; also, what about your children?"

"Margaret," I said, "three of my kids know that things are not right indoors as they're old enough. Whether they understand is another thing, but my baby, I'm worried about, as I know she won't understand now. One day I hope she will. Now, as for losing everything, no, I won't. I will have you."

Margaret looked at me and burst out crying. "Terry, I love you so much. Stop it – you have started me off." So we both sat there crying our eyes out.

We pulled ourselves together, and Margaret said, "It's getting late, would you like something to eat?"

I looked at my watch. It was nearly seven. "OK," I said. "I would like a quick sandwich, please." While Margaret was doing this I was thinking about what I would do next. The first thing to do was ring my friend Chas, who has a van hire company in north London, to see if he or any of his workers know where there might be a flat I could rent. Then once this had been sorted, I should see a solicitor. *God, this is going to be so nasty, knowing my wife and her mum and dad. Christ knows what my mum and dad are going to say.*

Margaret then came in with the sandwiches and coffee. While we were eating and drinking, I told her that I was going to Harrogate tomorrow night and staying up there then coming back the following evening, but I would pop in to have a kiss on my way up. She laughed, and with that, the door opened, and in came Ralph.

"Hi ya," he said.

"Ralph, I want to tell you something. Terry and your old mum," God, I was waiting and worried, "are in love with one another."

He laughed and said, "It's about time! You have been talking about him for the last six months, and he looks like a nice bloke." Then he gave me a heavy slap on the back and went upstairs to his room.

Margaret looked at me and said, "That's my Ralph." We both laughed and finished off the sandwiches.

I then said, "I will have to make tracks home."

"OK, but you drive steady. I know you're very happy, but watch the roads also. I hope it's not too bad indoors."

We both got up and walked to the door, embraced, and had a long kiss. I said I would see her tomorrow evening but would try to give her a ring at work during the day some time. We kissed again and said goodbye.

Driving home, I wondered what type of reception I was going to get – if any – as I had been out a long time to test a car, but I just didn't care. No man in this world could be as happy as me. My Margaret, yes, *my* Margaret, loved me and had done as long as I had loved her.

I got back to the house and waited for the music to start, and it did.

"Where the hell have you been? It don't take all this time to test a bloody car."

"I ran out of petrol and had to walk to a long way to a garage." *Why don't I just tell her the truth,* I thought, *as she is going to know soon.*

"I don't bloody well believe you. You have been seeing your fancy woman again."

"You believe what you want," I said and started off towards the back door to go to my studio.

"That's right, go and sit in your studio and drink gin, thinking of her."

I looked round at her and said, "What a good idea." I went out the door and unlocked my studio, still hearing her shouting and raving, and went in, locking the door behind me. Then, as she'd said, I got myself a very large gin, took a big mouthful – that felt good after all that raving I listened to – picked up the phone, and rang my friend to ask him if he knew of any flats going in north London.

"So you have been playing away then," he said.

"Shut up," I said. "When you find me a flat, I will tell you all about it."

"OK, babes," he said. "I will give you a ring and only talk to you if I find one."

I put the phone down, picked up my glass to have another swig, then I noticed some of my things had been moved; someone had been in the studio – but how? The door had been locked, and there was only one key, which I had. *Am I imagining this?* I checked in my filing cabinet; things were out of order in there. Yes, someone had been going through all my files and things. *What's there that could harm Margaret – come on, Tel, think.... the only thing is Margaret's work phone number, but there are also other lady clients' phone numbers. And there is nothing to say anything about my love for Margaret; the only thing is the drawing I did of her, but if you had never seen Margaret, you wouldn't know who it was, so I think there will be no threats. But how did someone get in,* I'm very puzzled.

I went up to bed and lay there trying to work out how anyone had gotten into my studio.

The next thing I heard was noises outside in the hall. It was the kids running about and getting ready for school and work. I lay there thinking about what had happened and what I had to do today. Knowing I was going to see Margaret that night lifted me. I got up and went out to my studio then rang the contractor in Harrogate to find out how the stand was going.

After I put the phone down, I went and got another cup of coffee and tried to speak to the wife, but she just walked out of the kitchen, so I went back in the studio and started work.

Just after lunch, my friend Chas rang and said he had heard of a flat in Hackney; he was going to have a look this evening and would ring later. I told him that I was going to Harrogate and would ring him the following day.

I finished the panels mid afternoon and rang Margaret to ask what time my love would be home. Margaret said about seven.

"OK, love, I will see you then."

Margaret blew a kiss and said, "I can't wait to see you."

I said, "Me too."

I put the panels in the car went back and locked my studio, still puzzled how someone got in, then went upstairs to change and pack.

After putting my case in the car I wrote a note of the hotel's phone number in case of emergency, put it on the table, and told the wife. She replied, "You don't think I will ring you if I need anything. You go off with your fancy woman and enjoy yourself."

I just said, "You think what you like." I got in the car, thinking, *That's it, it's on the fan, and it looks like it's going to get very nasty.*

I arrived at Margaret's street at about six thirty, so I popped in the pub at the bottom of the road to have a drink; in fact, I had two, sat till just after seven, said goodbye to the landlord, jumped in the car, and parked just past Margaret's house as there was a older green car outside.

I rang the bell and was greeted with a great big smacker and a cuddle. I went in, gave her another big kiss, and sat down. Margaret looked at me and said the day seemed so long. I laughed and said, "Me too."

Margaret asked me if I had eaten. "No," I said.

"OK, Ralph will be in soon. I will do a bit to eat then."

I asked if that was her car outside. "Yes," Margaret said, "I drive to the tube station every day."

With that, Ralph came in, said hi ya to us both, and gave me a whack on the shoulder, laughing. Margaret then went out to the kitchen to get the food ready.

After we had eaten, Ralph said he was going out to see his mate, and off he went. Margaret then asked me how things were going on at home. I told her what had happened and that someone had been in my studio, and I couldn't understand how, as I had the only key.

Margaret suggested the window. I said, "I thought that but checked them; they were still locked and had not been tampered with."

Margaret then said, "Your wife must have another key, I can't see that as there are only two; one I carry, and the other is in a drawer I keep all my drawing stuff in, and it's still there."

"Was there any chance of her getting it, getting one cut, then replacing it in the drawer when you may have left the door unlocked sometime?"

"I can't see that, as it would take time, but maybe." We carried on chatting. I was having a sneaky kiss now and then – mind you, there were no objections. Then I said, "By the way, who was that chap on Saturday?"

Margaret looked at me and laughed. "Why, are you jealous?" I shrugged my shoulders. Margaret laughed again. "That's my dancing partner. He's a married bloke but his wife can't dance anymore, so as a friend of theirs, I dance with him at the club round the corner; he picks me up and brings me home. Also, if we are early he comes in for a quick coffee. Does that answer your worries, my darling?"

"Yes, I expect so." Margaret then gave me a push, pulled me back, then I got a big smacker. "That was nice, can I have another?" Margaret obliged.

It was now about ten and Ralph came in, said "Hi ya both," then gave his friendly whack on the shoulder for me. Margaret just laughed.

"It's OK for you; you're not getting the whacking!" I looked at my watch and said, "I will have to push off," and looked at Margaret, as it was one of her sayings to me.

She looked at me and smiled, "OK, you win. Do you want a cup of coffee first?"

"No thanks, love, as I might have to stop on the M1, and I want to push straight through." I didn't want to leave but had to, so I got up. Margaret put her arm round my waist, squeezed me, and said, "Please drive careful, Tel." We walked to the door and kissed several times. I looked into her eyes; she was crying. "Don't," I said, "I will be OK."

"Alright," Margaret whispered. We kissed again, and I drove off with a big lump in my throat.

I arrived at the hotel at 2 p.m., very weary, a bit hungry, and wanting a good drink. I checked in with the night porter and asked, "Is there any chance of a drink and sandwich."

"I have a small stock of sprites miniatures. Also, I can do you a sandwich; what would you like?"

"A drink first," I said. "A gin if you have one."

"OK, would you like a tonic with it?"

"OK," I said. Up came the drink.

"What would you like in your sandwich?"

"A couple of rounds of anything."

A little later, back he came with the sandwiches, one cheese, one ham. "May I have a couple more gins, please?" I asked. I put the two little bottles in my pocket, grabbed the plate of sandwiches in one hand, with my bag and keys in the other, and went up to my room.

I woke about seven in the morning, as there was some noise outside in the room, possibly a rep. Off for breakfast, had a full house and ate the lot, went up to the room, got my bag, came down, and checked out.

I parked outside the hall to unload and had a bit of trouble with the parking bloke. Because I had a Jag, he thought I was an exhibitor. When I explained that I was delivering panels, he said I could have ten minutes and if I wasn't gone by then, I would get a ticket. I thanked him, knowing what I would have liked to say to him.

I took the panels to the stand, saw one of the contractors, said I would be back in a mo as I have to move the car or get a ticket.

"OK," he said, "but you better move yourself because that warden don't like cockneys."

I rushed back to the car just as the warden bloke was coming back. I said, "It's OK, I'm going now," and I sarcastically thanked him for his Yorkshire hospitality, got in my car, and went to the car park.

Back on the site, all was going well. There was still quite a bit to do but nothing to worry about yet. I looked at my watch; it was just after ten. Then off I went to find a phone.

I quickly dialled the number. "Hallo, Margaret Ensbury."

"Darling," I said.

"Tel, love, it's so—" Margaret stopped.

"What's the matter?" I said.

"It's alright. I'm just so happy to hear you. Now give me your number, and I will ring you back."

It seemed like hours before the phone rang, but when it did, I snatched it so fast I nearly dropped it.

"How is the stand going?" Margaret asked.

"Not too bad, but I would have liked it to have been a bit more ahead than it is. But no problem. Now I'm here, and I will do a bit of pushing."

"Now how are you, Tel?" Margaret asked.

"I'm OK but will be glad when I'm on my way home again later."

"Tel," she answered quickly, "don't drive back tonight if you're tired, please."

"I won't, my love, I promise."

Again she said, "Please, as you know I love you so much."

"Yes, my love, if I think I'm too tired I will stay up here."

"OK, but there is another promise I want you to make me. Please, Tel, don't drink if you're coming back tonight, promise."

"Margaret, I promise, so please don't worry."

"I really won't, thank you. I will save lots and lots of kisses for you."

"I want cuddles too," I said. She laughed and said goodbye.

I went back to the stand and said to the lads that I had just been onto the client (a little porkie), and he's a bit of a worrier, so I told him all was well. "So you won't let me down, will you? Also, there's £20 to go in your beer or tea kitty."

"OK, Tel, we won't let you down."

By late afternoon, the stand was nearly ready. The panels I'd done were all fixed, and there was just a bit of touching to be done. The client arrived and was pleased, but then he asked, "Terry, we have just brought in a new little machine. Can you get a plinth made for it, also a sign?"

"OK, leave it to me." I went over to the lads told them.

"OK, Tel, give us the size, and we will get it done."

Now for the sign. I didn't have my sign-writing kit in the car, so I asked one of the lads where the nearest art shop was. Off I went got a sheet of board and some Letraset. Then back I came. As I always carry a pen or pencil, tape, and a sharp knife with me, it was all systems go. The lads soon made the plinth, and while they were painting it, I did the sign. The client told us where he wanted the plinth to be placed, then I fixed the sign above it. All were well pleased. I shook hands with the client and left with the lads. I gave them their £20 and said, "See you again on site," and left to the nearest pub, as I was starving.

I went to the bar and was just going to ask for a large gin with a beer chaser when I remembered what I promised Margaret, so I asked for a pint shandy and a couple of ham rolls. I sat down and had a swig of the shandy – God, it was sweet and foul.

When I came out of the pub, I looked up at the sky. It was nice and bright. I had a good steady drive home. There was not a lot of traffic, but I tried to keep to the speed limit. It's hard when you're in a jag, there's a clear motorway, and you want to get home, so I did hit 90 a couple of times.

I finally got home about midnight. I went to the front door and put in my key. The door was bolted in the inside. I couldn't get in. *So what do I do now? If I start banging, I will wake the whole road up.* I decided to go back to the garage and sleep in the car. I found an old blanket that I kept in the garage to kneel or lie on when I was doing something to the car, got in, and covered myself up. I must have dozed off straight away, for I woke up freezing, then kept on sleeping, waking, sleeping, and waking till it was eight.

I went to the door and rang the bell. One of the kids opened the door, I said hallo, but got no answer. I went in the kitchen and said to my wife, "Why the hell did you lock me out? If you had listened to what I said, you would have known that I would have been home late, as I was working."

"Working! You were bloody lying. I rang the hotel yesterday morning, spoke to the receptionist, asked to speak to Mr Parker, and she said, 'You have just missed him, as Mr and Mrs Parker checked out just a while ago.'"

I just could not believe what she had just said, so I went to the phone, rang the hotel and asked for the manager.

"Who's calling?" the girl asked.

"Mr. Parker," I replied.

"Just a moment, I will put you through."

"Mr Parker, how can I help?"

I told him what had happened, he said "Just a minute." About three minutes later, he came back. "Yes, he said a Mr. and Mrs. Parker did check out, but there was also a Mr. Parker staying at the hotel, who checked out later. I'm sorry if there is any confusion."

"Thank you," I said. "Now please would you tell my wife?" I passed the phone over to her.

After about five minutes, she hung up and said, "You paid him to say that, so you can clear out when you like, as me and the kids don't want to see you no more. Just go and live with your fancy woman, if she will have you."

"Don't worry I will."

"The sooner, the better. Also, don't think I will do you food and washing while you're still here, because I won't."

I went out to the studio, slowly shaking my head, thinking about what had just happened and all what was going to happen, and I spotted something. The flap hinges on the studio door had been moved. My dad always told me that the sign of a good carpenter is that all the slots in the screws line up, so when I put them on I done this, but now some don't, that how they got into my studio, they took the door off.

I unlocked the door went in and first a large gin, then I rang Margaret.

"Hallo, Margaret Ensbury." Her voice was so marvellous to hear.

"Hi, my love, it's Tel."

Margaret screamed, "Tel, I have missed you so."

"Me too," I answered. Then I told her what had happened.

"How dreadful," she said. Then I told her that I had to ring my friend, as he was looking at a flat for me and would see her tonight.

"OK, I will cook you some dinner."

I thanked her, said must get on, blew a kiss, and hung up.

My next job to ring my mate Chas. "What's the hell is going on?" he said. "I rang you yesterday afternoon, your wife answered and told me to speak to your fancy woman."

"You know who she is", "Chas. I will tell you all about it when I see you. Now, any luck on the flat."

"Well it's a bit small, on the second floor, and the landlord owns the pub just a couple of blocks up."

"Can I see it this afternoon?"

"Yes, no problem. I will take you over there."

Now I needed to do a quick moving poster to send to all my clients. I could fill in the address and the phone after. *Christ knows how long will it take to get a phone connected. That's the first thing I must do when I know where I'm going to live.* I rang Margaret again and told her. She wished me good luck; also, Margaret told me that she could let me have a couple of towels, a bit of bedding, some cups, plates, pans, and such that she doesn't use anymore. I said, "You're a doll."

She laughed. "I know I am."

"And modest with it," I replied. We both laughed.

I roughed out a drawing with a car and trailer with a drawing board and filing cabinet, in the trailer, words about moving. But I just really couldn't concentrate, so I locked the studio and drove off to see my mate.

When I arrived, he said, "You're early, but we can go over the bloke's pub and have a drink so you can tell me what the fuck is going on." He drove me to the Hackney Road, and we went in the pub. We got some drinks, and I told him what was happening.

"What a fucking mess," he said. Mind you, he had been divorced and on his second wife. We had another drink and went to look at the flat.

It was a basic bedsitter, with a kitchen on the second floor. Outside on the landing was a toilet and a shower room, which had a little electric water heater. The ground floor was a minicab office.

I said to my mate, "It's not Buck house, but I will have it, as I want to get out ASAP." We went back to the pub, got another drink, and told the landlord that I would have the flat. He said OK and told me how much, two weeks in advance. I paid him there and then, and he gave me the keys, gave us both another drink, and said if I needed anything, to let him know. I thanked him and said I would move in on Saturday.

"OK," he said, "I will start the rent from Saturday." I thanked him.

On the way back to my friend's office, I asked if I could pick up a self-drive van on Friday night and return it Saturday night.

"No problem. I will get the form made out when we get back to the office."

When we got back I asked if I could use the phone to make a couple of calls. The first call was to the telephone people, and I asked how soon could they put me in a business phone at an address in Hackney Road. They said they could get one on Monday, and that was fine with me.

Next, I rang up Brian, another friend who had done some work for me in the past, and asked if he could give me a hand in moving some gear on Saturday.

"Yes, no problem," he said.

I said I would pick him up at 6.30 a.m. By then the form was ready for me to sign for the van and give a cheque. I sat there after this was all done, talking to my mate and finding out all about getting a divorce.

We sat chatting for about an hour. I said that I wasn't looking forward to all the hassle that would come, and he said, "Get yourself a good solicitor, as the courts always favours the woman, and you will come off worse."

"I will see you on Friday," I said and left.

I got to Margaret's street a bit early so went in the pub at the bottom of her street, got a drink, and sat buy the window so I could see right up the street and watch for Margaret to come home. It seemed like hours, then Margaret pulled up right outside her house. My drink went and I was in the car in seconds. I parked up and rang the bell.

Margaret said, "Hi, Tel, I have just got in." She had hardly finished and I was kissing her. I had her in my arms again; the world was marvellous with Margaret. She responded with another big kiss, then we just hugged. About five minutes later, Margaret said, "I must get the dinner ready. Come in the kitchen and tell me all about it. And did you get a flat?"

"Yes," I said. "I move in on Saturday, and the phone goes in on Monday."

"That's great, where is it?"

"The top end of Hackney Road, I would say about twenty minutes to a half-hour's drive from here."

Then Margaret said something that I hadn't thought of. "What about parking your car? Will you be able to park outside?"

I said, "I don't know. I will have to check it out on Saturday." We carried on talking about what had happened during the day, and then I said, "I nearly forgot. I know how someone got into my studio."

"How?" Margaret asked quickly.

"They unscrewed the flap hinges."

When dinner was nearly ready, I said, "There's an off-licence just down the road, next to the fish and chip shop, I will pop down and get a bottle of wine."

"OK, but hurry up as it's nearly ready." I was back in under ten minutes. Margaret dished up the dinner and brought it in the lounge.

"What about Ralph?" I said.

"He's gone round to a couple of older friends for dinner. He often goes there, as he does jobs for them. I think you are getting quite attached to him."

"Yes, I think he's a nice little chap."

"You know, he likes you a lot."

"That's good because I love his mum a lot."

"Shut up and eat your dinner."

Halfway through the dinner, I opened the wine. Margaret got a couple of glasses, I half filled them, and we said cheers and to good times to come.

After the meal, I helped Margaret to wash up. We came back to have another glass of wine, and Margaret said, "Where are you going to sleep tonight? You're welcome to sleep on the couch here."

I thanked her but said I would have to go back, as I had a lot to sort out tomorrow and needed an early start.

Margaret said OK then went out of the room. A couple of minutes later, she came back with two large blankets. "Take these in case you have to sleep in the garage again."

I looked and said, "Margaret, you are so thoughtful. I lo—"

She stopped me by putting her finger over my lips, and then said, "I will say it. I love you." Then she took her finger away and kissed me very passionately.

We sat for a while, and I said I would go soon, as I wanted to get an early start tomorrow. Margaret said, "I will make you a cup of coffee before you go."

While Margaret was making the coffee Ralph came charging, "Whatch ya," he said and came over and gave me my usual thump. "How are ya?"

"Not bad," I said. Then in came Margaret with the coffee. She offered some to Ralph, but he declined, saying he had to be up early tomorrow to go to market.

I took my time drinking my coffee, as I didn't want to leave Margaret. But I had to. Finally, the cup was empty and it was time to go. I stood up and looked at my lovely lady. She just dipped her head. "Please, darling, you take care. I'm so worried about you."

I got hold of her. "Don't worry, I will be alright." I kissed her, and she kissed me back. As I was leaving, she said, "Here, don't forget the blankets."

"Thanks," I said. I kissed her again, went out to the car, waved, and drove off.

I arrived home – which it wouldn't be for long – about eleven thirty. All the lights were out. I went over to the front door, and yes, it was bolted. I went back into the garage and got in the car, reclined the passenger's seat, wrapped myself in the blankets Margaret had thoughtfully given, and went to sleep quite quickly.

I woke up about seven. At first, I wondered where I was. I just lay there for a while, thinking and wondering what would be shouted at me when I went in the house; that's if I was allowed. But if she tried to stop me, I would tell her I would call the police, as it's still my house, for the mortgage is in my name.

I opened the house door, and Suzie ran upstairs. I said hi to Gary, and he mumbled. I didn't see Debbie or my wife. I made a cup of coffee and a couple of slices of toast. I went out, unlocked my studio, and went in, sipped at the coffee, and suddenly thought, *I won't be able to pick up the van on Friday night, as it won't go in the garage – where would I sleep?*

I rang the guy who was going to help me move and asked if he could hire a van on Friday night or Saturday morning. He said no problem if they had one free, as the hire place opened at 7 a.m. I could be at Sandridge in about half an hour from that. Then I had to ring Chas to cancel the van I'd ordered. When I told him, he said, OK, as the cheque didn't go in till I took the van back. "But you're a prat," he said. "It's your house; you should break in."

"What about the kids?" I said.

"Ya, I forgot about them. Let me know if you need any help."

I finished my coffee and rang Margaret. Her first words were, "Are you alright? Did you sleep OK?"

"Yes to both," I said.

"My love, thank God for that. I was so worried about you."

"Darling, I'm OK. Now can I see you tonight?"

"You better." She laughed.

"I will take you out for a meal."

"Don't be daft; you save your money."

"No, I insist."

"We will talk about it tonight."

"We won't have time, as I will be kissing you too much"

"Shut up," Margaret said, laughing.

"I will see you at the same time."

"OK, I love you," she said. She blew a kiss and hung up.

Before I could do anything more, I must go and have a shower, as I must hum a bit from sleeping all night in these clothes. I locked my studio and went in, where she was waiting for me.

"When you going? When and how will I get my money? And your father wants you to ring him."

"OK," I said, "I will be going on Saturday—"

"Good riddance."

"Can I finish? I will give you a months' money before I leave, then I will sort out proper payments when I have seen my solicitor."

"You better."

"Now, regarding me ringing my dad, that's my business when I ring him."

"I'm going to see my solicitor later, and you won't have anything. That will teach you to run around with all your fancy women," she said, and she then walked out of the kitchen. My mate had warned me it would get messy.

After she went out of the house, I had a nice shower, shaved, and put on some clean clothes. I was feeling a lot better. I went downstairs, and the washing was nearly done. When it was finished, I put in the tumble dryer and went in the studio to start packing some things. Suddenly the phone went; it made me jump.

"Terry." It was a strong voice on the phone. *Hell,* I thought, *it's my dad.* "What the bloody hell is going on?" he shouted.

"Don't shout, Dad," I said.

"I will shout if I want to."

"If you shout, I will hang up and leave the phone off the hook."

He calmed down and said, "What you doing boy?" All the family called me boy, never Terry.

"Things happen, Dad. We have been drifting apart for a long while now, and I fell in love with a lovely lady."

"Don't talk rubbish. You will forget about a young bit of skirt, and then where will you be?"

"Dad, the lady I am deeply in love with is older than me."

"You're serious, then?"

"Yes."

"What about the children?"

"Dad, Terrie's married and got her own life. Gary and Debbie are grown up now. Suzie, my baby, is the one I'm worried about, as she won't talk to me. Also, when she sees me, she runs away."

"What do you expect?" he said.

"Dad, it's over. I'm sorry, but this lady I have met I have loved for a long time, and before you say anything, there is nothing going on. Now I must go, as I have a lot to do. I will ring you early next week. Please explain to Mum for me."

"I will try, boy, but you know what your mum's like; she's doing her nut."

I said goodbye and hung up.

I went back in the kitchen, put my clothes in a case, and put it in the boot of my car. Then I went back into my studio, rang my solicitor, and got an appointment for mid-afternoon. I rang several of my clients and told them I was moving and they would get a letter about it with the new address and phone number. I decided to leave before my wife came back, as I didn't want any more shouting.

I locked my studio, drove into St. Albans, had a sandwich in a pub, with a couple of drinks, then went and saw my solicitor. We had a good chat. He said he would draw up some proposals for me to look at and asked where he could get hold of me when they were done. I said I would ring him next week when I have my new phone.

I left St. Albans and headed to Hackney to check on the parking outside the flat. It wasn't too bad, but I was a bit worried on leaving my jag outside all night. On getting out of the car, I noticed, opposite a church like hall, a house at the side, all in its own grounds with a big iron gate to go in. So I went over through the gate and knocked on the door. A nice middle-aged gent came to the door. I said good afternoon and explained my problem, then I asked him if there would be any chance of renting a small space, say for about £5 a week.

He had a quick think and then said, "I don't see why not; you can park just over there."

I thanked him very much and asked, "Shall I pay you now?"

"No," he said, "wait till you move in."

I thanked him again, shook his hand, and said goodbye, walking back to the car well pleased.

I was right off to see my Margaret. I went into the little pub down the bottom of the street as usual to get a drink and wait for my love to come home. The governor was getting to know me now.

"Hi again," he said. "Large gin and tonic?"

"Yes, please." I paid for the drink and asked him about a little restaurant about 200 yards away in Blythe road.

"It's very good," he said. "Slightly pricey, but good."

"Thanks," I said. "Please can I have the same again? Also, would you like one?"

"Thanks. Half of bitter."

We chatted a bit more, then I spotted Margaret's car come round the corner. I drank up my drink and said bye. He replied, "Have a nice meal."

I parked behind Margaret's car. The door was open, and I went in.

"Hallo, darling," Margaret said and gave me a big kiss. I wouldn't let her go.

"I want another." Margaret obliged. "You left the door open for me; how did you know I was here?"

"Saw your car outside the pub," she said and poked her tongue out at me.

"I'll bite it off," I said.

"You're welcome to try." We kissed again.

"What time would you like to go for the meal?"

"When you like. Where are we going? But you don't have to, I can do something," Margaret said, all in one breath.

"No, I want to make a fuss of you. I thought we would try that nice little restaurant round the corner in Blythe road."

"If you insist."

"What about Ralph?"

"Don't worry about him I will leave him out something; he eats anything as long as there is a lot of it." She laughed. "I will just go and clean up."

"OK," I said.

When Margaret came down, she had changed out of her working clothes and looked lovely. I told her so.

"Thank you, dear sir," she said, and out we went.

Margaret linked her arm in mine. I looked at her and whispered, "This reminds me of when I first took you out." We walked on a few more steps, and Margaret squeezed my arm and said, "I was very cruel to you that night, wasn't I?"

"No, love, you weren't cruel. I just surprised you by saying what I did."

Margaret squeezed my arm again. "I somehow knew because I felt the way you looked at me; also, every time we were together I wanted to kiss you, as I had fallen in love with you right from the start."

"May I ask you just one question?"

"Yes," Margaret said.

"Did your Rosemary know?"

"Yes, she had spotted it ages ago and told me to tell you how I felt."

"Why didn't you, then?"

"Because of your family. I was so worried it would hurt them."

"I told you that my marriage was on the rocks."

"It wasn't your marriage I was worried about; it was hurting your children."

I stopped, turned and kissed her, then said, "Thank you."

We arrived at the little restaurant and went to the little bar. We were met by a nice young man. "Good evening sir, madam."

"Good evening," we both answered. "I'm sorry, I haven't booked but have you a table for two?"

"Yes sir, if you would like to sit down, I will bring you over the menu. Would sir and madam like a drink?"

"Please. Two dry martinis with ice, please."

"Would that be with vodka or gin?"

"Gin, please."

The young man brought over the menu, went to the bar, made the drinks, and then brought them over. I thanked him then looked at Margaret, picked up my glass, and said, "To us." Margaret said and did the same. We clinked the glasses, sipped our drinks, then kissed. I looked at Margaret and said, "Margaret, you're a lovely, beautiful lady."

She laughed and said, "Tel, you have rose-coloured spectacles." Then she reached over and squeezed my hand, we then decided what we would like to eat. The young man came over and we ordered.

"Would you like some wine with dinner?" he asked.

"A bottle white, dry house, well chilled, please."

When our table was ready, we quickly finished our drinks and followed the young man downstairs to a lovely little dining room. It was just right, very intimate. The waiter brought up the wine and asked if I wanted to try it, no pour. We picked up our glasses, smiled, clinked them, and sipped. I looked at Margaret and said, "Are you happy?"

"Tel, I'm the happiest girl in the world. Also, Tel, I love you so much. You're my world, and I want to be with you forever. The way you look at me, I know you're the same."

I leant over and kissed her and heard, "Excuse me, sir." I broke away; it was the waiter with our dinner. "Sorry," I said, "but my lady wanted a kiss."

"No problem," he said, laughing, and he started serving our dinners.

After dinner, I asked, "Would you like a coffee and a brandy?"

"Just a coffee please."

So I ordered two coffees. The waiter bought them over with some after-eight mint chocks. As we sipped our coffees, I looked at Margaret and said, "I have something to say to you."

She started to laugh, and I said, "What's so funny?"

"Last time you took me out for a meal, you said that same thing after we had eaten," she said, and she carried on laughing.

I said, "Well, I hope I don't get the same answer as I did before."

Margaret laughed again and said, "So do I."

"Margaret, now be serious."

"OK, Tel," she said, trying to keep a straight face.

"Margaret, I then told you that I loved you." She looked at me, wondering what was coming next. "Now I'm going to tell you that when all my problems are sorted out, I'm going to ask you to marry me, and I will go down on my knee, if that's what I have to do to have you as my wife."

Margaret looked at me with big tears in her eyes and said, "Tel, the day you ask me that will be a day I will treasure forever and ever, for, Tel, you are the most wonderful and kindest man I have ever known. I love you with all of my heart."

I leant over, kissed her, and said, "You are also a very wonderful, lovely lady, who is not only my love but also my life." We kissed again and finished our coffees. I paid the bill, we thanked the waiter, and we started off home, arms round one another all the way.

We got in, and Ralph had gone to bed. I said to Margaret, "I won't get a bruised shoulder tonight," and she laughed. "I must push off – sorry, *move* off, as I don't like 'push off'. It brings back early memories."

Margaret laughed again. We had a couple more kisses and cuddles, and I said would give her a ring and see her tomorrow.

As I was driving down the M1, I realised forgot to tell Margaret that I'd found a place to park my car at the flat.

I arrived home as usual all in darkness. I don't know why I thought to try it, but I went over, put in the key, turned, and – bloody hell, she forgot to bolt it. I ran across to shut the garage door, went in, and tried not to make any noise. I checked that the room I'd been using was empty; it was, and I went to bed.

I woke early, just past seven. I didn't see anyone. So I drove to St. Albans and went in a café for breakfast. After I was finished, I went to the supermarket and bought stuff I might need at the flat: coffee, soap, toothpaste, kitchen rolls, paper hankies, and so on. On the checkout, I asked the lady if there were any cardboard boxes. She told me if I went round the back to see one of the chaps, he would give me some.

I went round the back and talked to a young chap; he pointed to a big pile of boxes and said, "Help yourself." I thanked him, folded and loaded about two dozen in my car, and drove back to my house. I was just going to put the key in the door when it opened and my wife came out.

She looked at me and said, "Tomorrow you're going?"

"Yes," I replied.

"Good riddance. And I want to know your address where you're living with your fancy woman."

I quietly said, "I will give you the address tomorrow when I leave, where I will be living *on my own,* as I know you will get your spies to confirm."

She carried on walking out, and I went in. I went up to the airing cupboard, got four towels (two hand, two bath), a couple of single sheets, a couple of pillow cases, a couple of kitchen towels, and a couple of blankets. I put them all in my car, took out the cardboard boxes, and went into my studio. I poured a large gin, picked up the phone, and rang Margaret.

"Hallo, darling," I said when I heard Margaret's voice.

"Tel, you OK? It's late, and I have been worried, as I haven't heard from you."

"Yes," I said. "I'm sorry, but I wanted to get out early to get some boxes to put my stuff in."

"Thank God for that," Margaret answered. Then we had a little chat about the night before and how lovely it was. I said I would see her tonight at the normal time, and I told her about getting a place to park my car.

"That's fantastic," she said. "Now you take care, as I want a nice big kiss tonight; also, don't worry about dinner as I'm going to do one of Ralph's favourites."

"I'm looking forward to it, and I will bring a bottle of wine."

"You trying to get your wicked ways with me?" Margaret asked.

I laughed and said, "One only can try!" She laughed, said "See you tonight," and blew a kiss.

I rang my friend to make sure all was OK for the following morning, then I got my address book out and rang all my clients and contacts to tell them I was moving and would give them details early next week. Also, I had two jobs outstanding, so I rang the two contacts to let them know; all seemed OK.

Then I had a sudden thought – answerphone. I rang the telephone company, gave them the contract number for putting in my new phone, and after a wait, a lady asked if she could help. I explained I was having a new phone put in on Monday morning, and asked if it would be possible also to have an answerphone unit. It was, but would cost extra. They would put it in when they put in my new phone.

I carried on packing up all my gear and records; there was a lot more than I thought. It must be hell when a big company decides to move. After I finished, I went up to my room and packed all my clothes. This part was hard, for as I was packing, I knew I was saying goodbye to my kids, who I love so much.

I packed everything except a change of clothes, razor, and toothbrush and paste. Still feeling very sad, I heard a door bang. *That must be her back,* I thought, so I took my cases down and put them in the studio with all my other gear and records. I locked the studio went in the kitchen and told my wife that a van to take all my stuff will be early tomorrow morning.

"The earlier, the better," she said, "and I hope you treat your fancy woman better than you have treated me."

I just said, "I tried my best, but for you, it wasn't good enough."

"You should have got a job instead of gallivanting all round the country with all your fancy women."

It was pointless to carry on talking to her, she had made up her mind, so I said, "I will give you a cheque for a month's money till I get a proper system sorted out."

"You better."

I just ignored her and walked out.

I drove to Hackney, took my car over to the little place opposite the flat, parked by the iron gates, and went to the house and knocked. The nice chap opened the door, looked at me, and said, "Hi ya."

"I have come to give you your first week's parking rent, as I will be moving in tomorrow."

"You could have left it till then," he said.

"No, I like to keep abreast of things." He took the £5, and then I went over to the pub to see the landlord and tell him I would be moving in tomorrow.

"OK, just a minute," he said, and he came back with my rent book and the keys. "Fancy a beer?"

"OK, half of bitter." He pulled a pint gave it to me, saying, "We don't do halves," and laughed.

I thanked him, finished my beer, and went to the flat street door. Before I went in, I went into the cab office and told the guy there that I will be moving in to the upstairs flat tomorrow morning.

"OK," he said, "if any of our cars are in the way, let me know, and I will get them moved." I thanked him and went up to the flat. I went in, and there was a medium-size room with a new single bed to one side of it, a chair, and a buffet-type wall about chest high leading in to a small kitchen area. I started to work out where I would put my drawing board (in front of the window) with my desk at the side. There was a double socket in the wall to the right. *Just right,* I thought, *once my board is in place I will juggle the filing cabinet in position.* I then sat on the bed and thought, *What a dump, but it will do for now till I get myself sorted out.* It was like starting all over again, but I had to do it. If I had stayed at home, it would have been terrible for the kids, seeing us shouting at each other, me being accused of carrying on with different women – this was so untrue; in fact, I used to keep the blokes in order on the tours.

What had happened to me, falling in love with Margaret, had just happened. I saw her, and that was it. I sat there for about half an hour, thinking of how I met Margaret, how I told her how much I loved her, how she told me to push off, and then the greatest day in my life, when Margaret said she loved me. I sat there crying.

I must pull myself together now; it's getting late, I thought, so got up quickly splashed some water over my face. I went downstairs and drove off to Hammersmith to see my love. I called in the pub at the bottom of the road, as usual, and soon Margaret's car came round the corner, I drank up and drove to Margaret's house.

"Hallo, Tel," she said and kissed me.

We went in the house. I said, "Just got to shoot out down the off-licence, as I have forgot the wine."

I got two bottles, one for tomorrow, and as I put them in the fridge, I asked Margaret what we were having for dinner.

"What's it worth?" she said.

"Big kiss," I answered.

"Payment first." So I paid my dues, then Margaret said, "Corn beef stroganoff on a bed of pillar rice."

"Sounds good," I said and gave her a little cuddle.

"Do you want your dinner or not? As you won't get anything if you don't let me go to start cooking it." We had a quick peck and I let her go, then I went in the front room to get out of the way. Seconds later, I went back into the kitchen.

"Now what?" Margaret asked.

"Would you like a glass of wine?" I asked.

Trying to keep a straight face, she said, "You're pushing your luck, and yes, please."

I poured out two glasses, gave one to Margaret, and said, "I will get out of your way now. Give us a kiss."

"Get out," she said with a grin.

"OK," I said and went again, but then I popped my head round the door and said, "Do you need any help?"

"You're really pushing your luck. Now push—" Margaret stopped. "Sorry," she said, laughing, "You know what I nearly said?"

"Yeah, I know. I'm naughty teasing you. I will let you get on." This time I went into the front room, put on the telly, and sat down with my wine.

About half an hour later, in came Ralph. "Watch ya," he said, giving me my normal slap on the shoulder. "How's it going?"

"So-so," I said.

"Mum cooking dinner?"

"It's your favourite."

"Good, beef strogs," he said.

A short while later, Margaret came in with forks and spoons, put them on the table, and said, "I'm dishing it up now."

"Good," said Ralph, "I'm starving."

"You always are," Margaret said, winking at me.

The meal was lovely, and I told Margaret so. "You would make a good wife for someone one day."

This bought a roar of laughter from Ralph, then he nudged me in the ribs and winked. I winked back, and he grinned then said, "Any more, Mum?"

"Yes," she said, "there is a bit left."

"Do want any more, Tel?" he asked.

"I'm OK," I replied.

After the meal, Ralph went out round to his mates. I went in the kitchen to help Margaret wash up and clear away. We did the jobs quite quickly and went back into the front room. I poured a couple of more glasses and sat next to Margaret.

"Everything OK for tomorrow's move?" she asked.

"Yes, I'm all packed and rearing to go. By the way, I have a couple of cases in my car. Please may I leave them here tonight?"

"Of course you can."

"I will get them now in case I forget." I brought them in and put them at the side of the TV out of the way.

"Now, Tel, you know I won't be in till later tomorrow evening, as I will be dancing at the club."

"Yes," I said. "You told me a few days ago. But can I still come over and see you for an hour when you get back?"

"Of course," she said, "I have got to have my goodnight kiss."

I leant over and gave her a kiss and said, "Have an early one now." Margaret kissed me back. I then said, "I will have to learn to dance."

"Really?" she said. Her eyes lit up. "That would be great. We would be able to dance together. I will ask at the club if there are any dance schools near you, in the Hackney area, where you may be able to learn sometime during the day, as daytime would be cheaper and no so busy."

"OK, sounds good to me."

We sat there chatting about my move the following day and how I thought it might go. I said I would just want to get loaded and on the road as soon as I could; I just didn't want any unpleasantness or nasty things being said. I would say nothing, just load up, say bye to the kids if I'm allowed, and go.

The move went well. The chap arrived on time, we loaded in about three hours, and I gave the chap the address and some directions and said I would follow shortly. Off he went. I went into the lounge, gave my wife an envelope with her money and the address was on it.

"Off to live with your fancy woman now, then." she said.

I just replied, "You think what you like," and walked out. She shouted something to me, but I didn't hear what it was. I got in my car and drove off.

I parked up right outside of the flat, what a bit of luck, and I went into the cab office and asked if I could use the phone. "No problem," the bloke said.

I rang Margaret. "Is that you, Tel, are you alright? I have been so worried."

"Take a breath, love," I said.

"Are you alright?"

"Yes, no problem, all went well. I'm just waiting for the van to arrive."

"OK," she said, "I will let you get on. See you later tonight, about 9.45 p.m."

"I love you."

"Thanks, darling, I love you too. Bye." I hung up to an "aww" from the drivers in the office. I just laughed and walked out. Ten minutes later, the van pulled up. I drove over to the parking place I had opposite, so the van could park in my spot. I said to my mate, "Let's go for a beer and something to eat before we unload."

Half an hour later, we came back and started to unload, and that was something else. The boxes were no problem, but the filing cabinet, desk drawer unit, and drawing board were trouble getting them up the small staircase. There were a few nice words said, but we finally did it. I paid my mate Brian, and he thanked me and said, "This is a bit of a comedown, Tel."

"Yeah, I know, but it's only temporary till I sort myself out."

"Good luck, and if you need any help with the tours or moving, give me a bell. See ya." And he left.

Right before I start to sort things out, I must go and get some food, and also, more important, some booze. I was out about an hour and came back with some tins, rolls, margarine, cheese, gin, and lager. I opened one of the lagers, took a good swig, and started to put things in place. *God, this flat is a lot smaller than I thought.* It took me a good two hours to do it, plus another lager and three or four gins. I then sat on the bed and thought, *Tel, you have now got to start to sort yourself out. First start eating properly again; you have lost a massive amount of weight. You have had to buy new clothes, as your others just hung on you. Also, you have broken all your own laws about drink; you have always said you must eat if you want to drink, but you have been living on gin. It won't be long before you become an alky; then you will lose the lady of your life.*

God, I thought, *I must stop. When I see Margaret later, I must ask her.*

I must have sat there for an hour or so, just thinking, *God, if I lost her, life would not be worth living, then I* would *become an alky.*

Now I thought, *Got to clean myself up. I will try the shower out.* It was one of the pay-as-you-go, taking ten pence. On the gauge it showed there was about twenty minutes, so I put in thirty pence, went in, and had a shower. It was OK – nothing to write home about, but OK. I went back to my flat, had a shave, brushed my teeth, and got dressed. I looked at my watch; it was ten to nine. I locked up my flat and drove off to see Margaret. I couldn't wait.

As I went into the house, Margaret grabbed me, pulled me to her, and kissed me very hard and passionately. Margaret said, "Tel I have been so worried about you. I really didn't want to go dancing, but I thought it would take my mind off things. It didn't, and I danced terrible. I just kept thinking of you. I know you said all went well, but I was still worried."

"Truly, it was OK, but getting the stuff upstairs was a bit of a problem."

She cuddled me again and said, "Would you like a cup of coffee? Please, go and sit down, and I will bring one in."

She brought the coffee in, put it on the coffee table, and was just going to say something when I pulled her to me and kissed her for about five minutes. Margaret looked at me and said, "Our love will never die." Then kissed me again. We sat there chatting about my move and laying out my stuff. Then I told her that I had something to say to her.

She laughed and said, "You have already said that, in a restaurant in Birmingham."

I laughed and said, "No, I want your honest advice."

Margaret looked puzzled. "OK," she said, "Fire away."

"Do you think I drink too much?"

Margaret took hold of my hand and said, "Tel, I know you have been under enormous pressure, but yes, I think you drink far too much gin. You know how much I love you, so I was going to say something once you had moved out."

I kissed her again and said, "I'm going to pack up drinking for a month, then after that, just have a beer or a glass of wine, but no spirits for a long, long while."

"Tel," she said, "you won't find it easy to do."

I took a long look at her and said, "Margaret, I have you for support."

She whispered, "You know you have my love." We were just going to kiss when the door burst open and in came Ralph. "Hi, Mum and Tel," he said, with the usual thump on my shoulder, "how's it going?"

"OK," I said.

"What about the move, did that go well?"

"Yes, no problem," I answered.

"Good. I'm going to do a sandwich, do you lovebirds want anything?"

"No," we both laughed.

We carried on talking for about another half-hour, then I said I had better get going, as I was feeling a bit tired, and if it was nice tomorrow, I could pick her up and go out for a ride somewhere.

"Yes, that would be lovely," Margaret said. "Also, if you get here about 11.30 we could have a light lunch first."

"I might be a bit earlier than that so I can have a kiss first."

Ralph burst out laughing, "You're like one of the kids in the youth club," he said, then we all started to laugh. I got up.

Margaret said, "You off now, then? I will see you to the door." As we walked out, Ralph shouted, "Don't forget to kiss him, Mum."

Margaret shouted back, "Push off!" Then she said to me, "Ooh, I'm sorry, darling!"

"It's OK, you didn't say it to me." We had a couple of kisses, said see you tomorrow, then Margaret said, "Hang on, I nearly forgot the bedding." She ran upstairs and bought down some bedding she had sorted out for me. I thanked her and left, tired but very happy.

The flat seemed a lonely place; still, it was better than the garage. I sat on the bed to take off my shoes and could hear quite a bit of noise outside in the street. I went to the window and looked out; about half a dozen blokes and girls had all had a bit too much and were shouting at one another. I thought how pleased I was to have my car in the little place over the road behind gates.

I came back to the bed and started to get undressed when I heard someone go past my door then upstairs to the top flat, ah that must be the long distant lorry driver the landlord had told me about, I got into bed turned out the little side light I had bought with me.

I woke early the following morning; first I wondered where I was, then I got up, made a cup of coffee, and had a look out of the window. I looked across the road and saw the car. All seemed OK. I felt a bit cold, so I looked through my change to find some ten-pence coins for the meter. I put some in and turned on the electric fire, made myself another cup of coffee, and toasted a roll in front of the fire. While I was eating the roll, I went to my desk to see what work I had in hand. I sorted out which was the most urgent and put them in order. *God, I could do with a drink*, I thought, *but no, I have got to stop*. Then I thought, *Just one – no! What is the most important thing in my life? Yes, Margaret, so think of her and be strong.*

Then I heard the chap upstairs coming down, so I went out to say hallo. He seemed a nice chap. He said he was a driver and just on his way to work, so we said our goodbyes, and off he went.

I got to Margaret's just after ten, and Ralph opened the door. "Watch ya," I said and thumped him on the shoulder. He laughed. "Hi, Tel. Mum's in the kitchen."

I walked in and gave her a peck on the cheek. "Is that all I get?" she said.

"But you're busy," I said.

"That's no excuse." So I grabbed her and gave her a big kiss. "That's better," she said. "Would you like some egg and bacon?"

"Yes, please," came a loud voice from the hall.

"OK, Ralph. I know you're there." Margaret laughed. After ten minutes, in she came with two plates of egg and bacon, then she went out to get hers and the bread.

"What about the sauce, then?" Ralph said.

"You know where it is," she replied.

Ralph got up, winking at me, mumbling something about having to work for your supper.

After we had finished, I collected the plates and took them out to wash up. Ralph said, "You've got him well trained, Mum," and he laughed.

I came back, and as I sat down, I asked Margaret if there was anywhere she would like to go.

"We could take a run out towards Richmond way and find a little place by the river, and you can tell me all about your flat."

"That sounds nice," I said, "but there is not much to say about the flat. It's just a place to work and sleep."

I got out my map to check what route to take, then off we went. I drove for about half an hour, and we spotted a little pub with seats outside by the side of the river. I pulled up and asked, "What do you think?"

"Looks OK. Let's give it a go."

We started chatting about the flat, and I told her about finding somewhere to do my dyelines for me. She felt there must be somewhere near. We sipped our drinks, and I asked if she had found out about dancing schools in Hackney. She had forgotten to ask, but said she would ask on Tuesday when she next went to her club.

We had one more drink and chatted away for quite a long time. Then we got up, held hands, and walked along the river for a while. We decided we had done enough walking and wandered back to the car. We sat in the car, and Margaret said how she enjoyed a nice lazy afternoon. I felt well relaxed.

As soon as we got back, Margaret put the dinner on. I asked if she needed any help.

"No," she said, "I'm OK, but I will need a kiss when I come in."

"Don't know about that," I said.

Margaret answered, "Ooh, playing hard to get are we?" About ten minutes later, she came in and jumped on my lap, saying, "What's all this about, 'I don't know about that'?" I pulled her towards me and kissed her passionately. "Tel, that was lovely. Please, can I have another?

I obliged. Still on my lap, she sat chatting away for a good while, then got up to into the kitchen, saying, "Ralph will be in soon, as he's never late when he knows there is grub going."

And she was right; five minutes later in he came, shouting, "Home, Mum and Terry, then came over and gave me my normal whack.

After dinner we didn't do much, just watched telly till it was time for me to leave. Ralph had gone to bed, as he had to be up early for work. Margaret walked with me to the door. We kissed and cuddled. "You drive safely now, and don't forget to ring me as soon as you're on the phone."

"OK," I said, gave her another big kiss, got in the car, and drove off.

Driving home, I realised I hadn't had a gin all day and didn't want one, but I wasn't on my own. I didn't think it would be so easy when I was in the flat.

I was right. About ten minutes in the flat, I badly wanted a gin. I went over to my bottle. It was just over half full. I picked it up, but then I could hear Margaret saying, "Yes, I think you drink too much gin."

I went over to the sink and poured it away, saying, "See, Margaret, I have listened to you my love."

I woke early the next day and made a cup of coffee. While that was cooling, I went to a little café three doors along and got a couple of ham rolls. I sipped at my coffee, *God, I really could do with a drink; its hell.* I took a bite out of the roll. I really didn't want it. I only wanted a drink. Another sip of coffee and another bite of roll. This was so hard. *Right, let's get on the drawing board and try to do some work,* I thought. I started to rough out a design, had a drop more coffee. It was nearly cold. I ate some more roll and was now really feeling rotten. Then the bell went. The phone man – I had forgotten about him. I rushed down the stairs. Yes, it was the phone man. He came upstairs and asked where would I like it. I showed him and offered him some coffee. Two cups for him and one for me. I went back to my board and started to work again, feeling a little better, but still rough.

About three hours later, he said, "OK, you're now on the phone." He then ran through how the answering worked with me. It seemed simple enough to work, so I thanked him and signed his sheet. He went down and got my phone books, and I thanked him again, gave him a couple quid for a drink, and said goodbye.

I then quickly rang Margaret to give her the number. Rosemary answered and told me that Margaret was in a meeting, so I gave her my number to ring me back also. I said to Rosemary that I had a bone to pick with her next time I saw her.

She laughed and said, "I wonder what that can be?"

"You know," I said. She laughed. "When did you know how I felt about Margaret?"

"A long time before you told her that you loved her in the restaurant in Birmingham. You wear your heart on your sleeve."

"And how do you know about what I said in the restaurant?"

There was a pause. "Well... But you promise not to say anything?"

"Yes, I promise." When Margaret came back to the hotel from the restaurant, she knocked on my door and asked to talk to me. I said yes, thinking there was a problem with the stand. She came in and was crying. 'What's the matter, Margaret?' I asked her. She looked at me and said, 'That silly Terry has just told me he loves me.' I looked her and said, 'What's the problem? You love him.' 'How do you know that?' Margaret said. I just said that you couldn't be a close secretary without knowing your boss. I look and listen. I told her, 'Margaret, follow your heart. Terry is a very kind, loving gentleman, and I can see in his eyes, he really loves you so much—"

"That's very kind of you to say," I said.

"Terry, that's OK, but it's true. Also, you and Margaret are the happiest lovers I have ever seen; you are just one person. Terry, you are made to be together, and I know you will marry and love one another for the rest of your lives."

I tried to thank her, but found talking hard. I managed to say, "You are a very wise lady, and forget the bone I had with you."

She laughed and said, "When you do marry our Margaret, you look after her, as she is one of the most wonderful ladies you will ever know."

"I know, Rosemary," I said, "And yes, Margaret is my life, and I will cherish her forever."

"I know you will, Terry, and I will get Margaret to give you a ring."

I was crying my eyes out. *Must get a drink – no drink. Big problems, God I need a drink – make some coffee. Sod the coffee, I need a drink, I must go out and get one.* I put on my coat and went to the door, but then I heard Margaret's voice, "Yes, I think you drink too much gin."

I stopped, took off my coat, and sat on the bed. I was in a very bad way, shaking, dry mouth. I tried making more coffee. While it was cooling, I went to my board and tried to draw, but I was shaking too much. Back to the coffee. I drank a drop and burnt my mouth. *This is hell,* I thought. Then I jumped; the phone rang. I picked it up and slowly said, "Hallo?"

"Tel, is that you?" It was Margaret.

"Yes," I answered.

"You alright, Tel?"

"Not really."

"What's the matter, darling?"

"I need a drink, Margaret."

"Have you eaten?" she asked.

"Had a roll about eight."

"Tel, please, for me, don't drink."

"Margaret, I love you, I promise."

"Right, you get in your car and come home to me. I will leave early now. Don't worry, they owe me a lot of time, and Rosemary can take care of things."

"OK, love, I will leave straight away. I promise, no drink. I love you too much."

God, I thought, *I haven't showered or shaved.* I rushed into the shower but forgot to put any money in, so halfway through it went cold. That sorted me out quickly – must remember that – I had a quick run round with the razor, a couple of cuts, chucked on some clothes, and off I went.

I parked up just outside Margaret's house; her car was already there. As I got out, she came out and got hold of me, took me indoors, and cuddled me. "Tel, are you OK?"

"Yes, I'm alright now. You're with me."

She kissed me hard. "Tel, I will always be with you." I just squeezed her. "Margaret, I love you so much. Without you, life is not worth living."

"Now Tel, come on, this is not you to be so down, after what you have been through. Yes, I know to pack up this drinking problem will be hard, but you can make it."

Tuesday I rang round to all my clients, giving them my new phone number and generally having a chat. This was helping my drinking withdrawal problems, keeping my mind busy. Also, the client I did the tours for said, "Don't forget, I want you to run the office and drawing equipment show in Manchester later in the year."

"OK," I said, "no probs."

I saw Margaret late that evening, as she went to her dance club. She told me that there was a dance school near me in Hackney, and if I would like to have a look she would come with me on Saturday. I said that would be great; also, I could show her my flat.

The rest of the week didn't go too bad. I started working a lot better but still had some withdrawal problems. I was managing to eat a couple of rolls during the day but drinking a lot of black coffee. Going over to Margaret's every evening was just marvellous, but on Friday a big thing happened in both our lives.

I arrived at Margaret's about seven. I had already told her that I was taking out to a little pub for dinner. The pub was just a bit too far to walk, so we jumped in the car about half past seven, drove round to it, and had a nice meal, taking our time to enjoy the evening also no work tomorrow. When we got back, Margaret had coffee in the front room. She kissed me and said thank you for a lovely evening.

Ten minutes went by and in came Ralph. "Hi ya both," he said, and I got my usual thump. He went out to the kitchen, and Margaret said, "He's hungry again." Back he came with a thick sandwich and coffee, and we all sat watching the telly. When Ralph finished his grub and coffee, I looked at my watch and said I had better be off.

Then it happened: Ralph said, "Why don't you sleep here?" I just didn't know what to say.

Then Margaret said, "What a good idea. I will go up and get a pillow, also some blankets, and make a bed up on the couch."

Then Ralph said, "Mum, what do you want to do that for, as you have a double bed in your room?" Then he laughed, said good night, and went up to bed. I was now in a deep form of shock.

Margaret looked at me with her big loving eyes, took hold of my hand, and said, "Well?" I just looked her. I had a big lump in my throat and tears in my eyes, but I just couldn't speak. I pulled her to me, and we kissed very passionately.

The following morning at seven, there was a knock on the door. We were still cuddled together. In came Ralph with a tray, two coffees, and a plate of cheese crisp bread and tomatoes. He put it on the little table at Margaret's side of the bed, and said, "Good morning, I have made you a continental breakfast, and I'm off to work now. See ya both tonight." He got halfway out of the door and turned. "You look good together," he said and went. Margaret looked at me and said, "That's my Ralph."

We drank the coffees then cuddled up together, both feeling so, so happy. I went to say something, but Margaret put her finger over my lips, smiled, took it away, then kissed me.

About an hour later, we got up took the tray of food down to the kitchen and ate it with another cup of coffee. "What time do we have to go to the dance school?" I asked.

"They open about eleven," Margaret replied.

"After we could go down Ridley market and have a look round if you fancy it."

"That will be nice," Margaret said. "I can get all my week's shopping, now I have a guest staying with me."

I laughed and said, "You never know one day that guest might ask you to marry him."

Margaret stopped what she was doing, looked at me with those great big beautiful eyes, smiled, and said, "Maybe someday he will."

"I wonder what you would say."

Margaret giggled and said, "You would have to wait and see."

"Come here and give me a kiss." And she did.

Off we went to find the dancing school in Hackney. We found the club; it was above a big shop. We walked into a big hall with about thirty very young kids in there, I looked at Margaret and said, "I'm out of here, look at all those kids."

"Shut up," Margaret said, "they are not interested in you. They are learning themselves."

I wasn't impressed. A lady came over and asked if she could help. Margaret told her that I would like to learn basic social dancing. The lady said it would be no problem. She also said not to worry about the kids. "They have their own problems, as they are all taking their medals this week."

Margaret laughed and said, "I told you so," so I made a booking for the following Tuesday afternoon. But then Margaret said, "What about now?" I could have killed her.

"OK," the lady said, "we will have an hour on the waltz."

Margaret sat down, and I followed the lady over to the far side of the hall, feeling a right fool. The lady then put on some music and off we went. The lady had a lot of patience, but after about half an hour I started to respond.

After I finished, Margaret said, "You done well," and gave me a peck.

"If you say so, but if I get better, will I get a bigger peck?"

"Shut up, you randy old bugger. Let's go and do a bit of shopping." So off we went to the market. After we had finished, Margaret said, "Are we going back to your flat now?"

We went back to my flat, and I offered her some coffee. I made the coffee while Margaret looked round. "It's a bit small, but it's OK. Now Tel, how do you send and your invoices and things?"

I looked at her, a little puzzled. "What do you mean?"

"Where's your typewriter?"

"I haven't got one. I write all invoices by hand."

"Right," she said. "You will now bring all your paperwork over to me, I have an old typewriter and will do all your invoices for you."

"Margaret," I said, "you work all day."

"Now you listen, Tel. You have to get yourself sorted out. You have packed up drinking spirits, so now you are going to look after the business. We – yes, we – have a new life together, so let's go for it."

"Margaret, I just don't know what to say. You're just such a wonderful lady."

"Tel, I love you, and I'm going to help you. You're a lovely bloke, and you deserve to start earning on the wonderful talent you have, which you haven't done so far – trust me."

I embraced her and kissed her gently. "Margaret, I love you so much" and started to kiss her harder, we broke off, Margaret said, "I know, Tel," gave me a little kiss, and said, "later." I picked up all my paperwork and we left the flat.

When we got back to Margaret's house, I asked if I might use her phone, as I had forgotten to give my mum and dad my new phone number. She said it was no problem, as she was going to get the dinner ready.

My father answered. "You alright, boy?"

"Yes, OK, and very happy."

"Good, now your mother wants to talk to you." The way my dad said that, I knew the she was going to have a go at me.

"What the bloody hell do you think you're doing?" And she just kept going on.

"Mum—" I tried to speak, but she still kept going on.

"Mum, if you don't let me speak, I will hang up. She stopped. "Now you listen, Mum. When I was a little lad about ten, I came home from school, and there was a man in the front room. You told me it was Uncle Albert. As I got older, I found out that I didn't have an Uncle Albert."

"That was a long time ago; also, there was nothing in it, but you have left your home and family for other women."

"Right, first," I said, "it's not other women. Second, things have been going wrong for a long time at home, and third, I have fallen in love with a wonderful lady."

"All I can say is I hope you know what you're doing, as you will be the loser, and things will get nasty."

"I know, Mum, but this lady is my life." I then gave her my phone number and said goodbye.

After dinner, Ralph got the typewriter down from upstairs, said "See ya later," gave me a thump and went out.

"You should tell to stop doing that, Tel."

"No, it's just a bit of fun. He's a good lad."

Margaret got an old toothbrush and started to clean the typewriter, then I put a little drop of oil in the moving parts.

"Right," said Margaret, "let's see if it still works." She put in a sheet of paper and started to type.

"Bloody hell," I said, "You're fast."

She just laughed and said, "Not as fast as I used to be, because Rosemary does most of my typing now. OK, let's go through the invoices you have to send."

"But Margaret," I said, "I haven't designed or got printed any letterhead paper yet."

"Don't worry I will put in a temporary one and explain."

"Margaret, you're marvellous," I said.

"Yes, I know." She laughed. I gave her the details, and she started bashing away on the typewriter.

"I will go and get a bottle of wine," I said. Margaret just waved her hand. When I came back with a couple of bottles of wine, Margaret was still bashing away on the machine. I said, "Stop a minute, and have a wee glass." I poured a couple of glasses.

Margaret sipped hers and said, "You sign these invoices, please, and I will stamp and post them tomorrow; also, I have a couple more to do after I have had this break, and you can look up in the yellow pages to find a local printer."

"OK, love," and before I had finished speaking, she was typing again. I looked in the phone book, found a couple of printers that looked likely, and wrote them down. Then I picked up one of the invoices Margaret had typed. "Margaret," I said.

"Hang on a minute, I'm just finishing the last one."

When she had finished, she said, "First I will have another glass, as I think I deserve it."

I poured two more glasses. Margaret had a good drink and then asked, "What do you want to say, darling?"

"The invoices, I think they are too high."

"Rubbish, Tel. You have been undercharging yourself. You are a very reliable, skilful, artist designer, so now you're going to charge the right prices. Trust me, I know, so don't worry. Also, you will need as much money you can get when your settlement comes out. Tel, my poor darling, you're going to have a rough time, but I'm here to help you, so let's get another glass of wine and take it up to bed with us."

I, as a good boy, poured the drinks and followed Margaret up to bed. She was already in bed wearing, as usual, her nightdress, Calvin Klein. I put Margaret's drink on the little table at her side, sipped a little drop of mine, and put it on my little table. I undressed and got into bed, saying to Margaret, "Aren't going to have a sip of your drink?" She pulled me towards her, kissed me, and said, "Later."

The following couple of weeks seemed to fly past. I was still having withdrawal symptoms, but it was getting better. I started to go for dancing instructions for an hour two afternoons a week and going to my lodge for instruction on learning the ritual. While I was at the lodge, I had a chat to one of my brothers, who had a flat in Malta, and asked him if he still let it out, and if so what dates were available. He wrote down some dates, and I said I would give him a ring and come over to see him one weekend at his pub.

Work was coming steady, and I was the happiest I had been for a long time, despite the aggro with solicitors' letters flying about. I also found a very helpful father-and-son printing company who did my letter heading very quick and at a good price. Margaret wall doing all my paperwork in the evenings, so I used to help by doing the cooking.

One evening after dinner, we were having a cup of coffee, and I said to Margaret. "I want to ask you something."

She burst out laughing. "Here we go again."

"No, be serious," I said.

"Alright," she answered giggling.

"Would you like to go away for a week's holiday to see if we would still love one another as much when we are together all day for seven days?"

"Tel," she said, "my love for you is forever, but are you worried about yourself?"

"God no, Margaret, I love you so much. I just thought it would be lovely. As usual, I have cocked up what I mean."

"No, I know what you mean, love, and yes, it would be marvellous. I have a lot of leave owing. You let me know so I can book it."

"Right, have you got a valid passport?"

"Yes, why?" Margaret said with an exited voice.

"How would you like to go to Malta, as one of my Masonic friends has a flat he lets out?"

"Oyo, Tel, that would be fantastic." She gave me a big cuddle.

"If I tell you all that again, do I get another big cuddle?"

"Shut up," she said laughing.

"Right, next Saturday we will go over to his pub and see him. He's a great chap you'll like him."

"Can't wait," Margaret burbled out and gave me a kiss.

"About time," I said, and she gave me another.

That Saturday, about eleven in the morning, we set off to my friends pub in Hertfordshire, I had already rang him on the Friday evening to let him know we were coming. He told me that he couldn't wait to meet this lovely lady of mine.

We pulled into the pub car park. There were a couple of geese and a goat running round on the grass by the side of the park, and one of his lads was out feeding the geese. Margaret said, "Do I look OK?"

"Of course, darling," I said.

"I'm a bit nervous, as it's the first one of your friends I'm going to meet."

"Don't be silly; he's a great friendly bloke. You'll love him, you'll see." I got out and opened the door for Margaret. The lad came over and said hi, and so did the bloody goat. It tried to butt me, to great roars of laughter from Margaret and the lad. I got Margaret in the pub quickly. My friend came round from the bar, shook my hand, and said hi.

"What's the matter with the bloody goat of yours? It tried to have a go at me." My friend and Margaret both started to laugh. "It wasn't funny," I said.

When they stopped laughing I introduced Margaret to my friend. He shook her hand, kissed her on the cheek, and said to me, "How did a ugly old bugger like you get such a lovely lady like Margaret?"

We all laughed, and I thought, *Yes, how did I get such a beautiful loving lady?* My friend said to Margaret, "What would you like to drink?"

"A small lager, please."

"And you dreamer?" I was still thinking about Margaret.

"Oh, the same please."

He went round the bar and served the drinks. I went to pay, but he said, "No, that's on the house." He joined us with half of Guinness, and we all chatted to one another between him serving other customers. Then his lady came down, and there were more introductions. She took over, and he came round to talk about the flat. We said when we would like to go, and he said to let him know once we had a flight booked, and he would make all the arrangements.

On the way back, Margaret said, "You were right; he is a nice chap, also a gentleman."

"Like me," I said with a straight face.

"Yeah, if you like, but you're all allowed to your own opinions. No, darling, I'm only joking. You are a very kind gent."

When we got home, Margaret said she would book a week's leave. As soon as she knew it was OK, she would ring me. Once I knew, I would go to a travel agent to see what flights are available.

"Tel, it will be lovely all on our own in the sunshine, making love with only a sheet over us, and local wine to drink after."

"How do you know it will be that warm?" I asked.

She laughed. "If it's not we will make it warm."

"Margaret, you're wicked."

"Yes, darling I know, but you wouldn't like me any different."

I replied, "The fifth amendment."

"OK, I accept what you say, but are you going off me? I haven't had a kiss for a long while."

"I didn't think you were hungry."

"I will show you how hungry I am." Margaret then came over pulled me to her and said, "Now let's see how hungry you are."

We got up quite early on Monday morning, as Margaret wanted to book her leave and get it accepted ASAP. I got to my flat, found a letter from my solicitor, also a couple of cheques. I thought Margaret typing out the invoices seemed to be working. I felt I needed a drink before I opened the solicitor's letter, but I did not, so I made a cup of coffee instead. While it was cooling, I went to the café and got a couple of ham rolls, came back had a sip of the coffee, and took a bite into one of the rolls. The phone went. *Good, it's Margaret with the dates.* It wasn't; it was a company who I had been recommended to. They had booked space in a forthcoming building exhibition at the NEC and asked if I would be interested in submitting a design.

I said I would and made an appointment to see them. I was quite pleased, as I hadn't done a stand in the building exhibition since I'd been on my own. Again, I would have liked a drink, but no; I had coffee. As I was finishing my half-eaten roll, the phone went again. It was my Margaret.

"Yes, love?" I asked, "have you a date for your leave?" She gave me the dates. "Right, I will go and see if I can get a flight."

"OK, darling," she said, "but please let me know ASAP, for I'm so excited."

"OK, my love, I will. But what's it worth?"

"You will find out later." She blew a kiss and said goodbye.

I ate my second roll, threw away my second cup of coffee, and went out to find a travel agent. I popped in the pub and had a half of lager (fancied a gin but didn't have one), and I asked about a travel agent. There was one about 100 yards on the right towards the church. I drank my lager, thanked the barman, and left.

The barman's directions had been spot on. I got a flight from London Airport on Air Malta arriving in Malta at four thirty in the afternoon and returning to Heathrow seven days later at ten thirty in the evening. I rang my Margaret, and she was over the moon. She said, "Darling, this is going to be such a wonderful holiday – love, sun, a little wine, and more love under a sheet. Tel, I'm such a lucky lady to have you."

"Margaret, just remember the restaurant months ago and what I said – I meant it, and I still do love you and will forever."

"Tel, I know we are so lucky to have this love for each other; many think they have love, but they haven't. Rosemary is so happy for us, but she's a little envious. I don't care. I will give you my happiness tonight when we are together."

The weeks that followed seem to drag, as we were both so excited about going on holiday together. Margaret kept saying, "We can cuddle and kiss all day and all night if we want to." I must say, Margaret did love her cuddles; mind you, I didn't object to giving her them.

At last the day came. We got a taxi and arrived at the airport nice and early, checked in, and went to the duty free shop to get a good supply of the menthol cigarettes we both smoked. The we went into the depart lounge for a drink. We were like two silly young kids, excited and in mad love. I got a couple of lagers, and we sat to wait for our call, praying there would be no hold ups. The time seemed to be going slower and slower, then at last we were ask to board. Off we went.

Soon after, the hostess came round asking if the passengers would like a drink. I looked at Margaret; she knew what I was going to say and beat me to it, "Yes, you can have a gin and tonic and ice but not gin on its own."

"Do you think it will be OK?" I asked.

"Yes," Margaret said, "as you haven't had a sprit for nearly two months now and you don't crave for it anymore. But take it easy."

So when the lady came to us, I ordered two gin and tonics with ice. We poured our drinks, said cheers, had a kiss, then we both sipped our drinks. I must say the gin and tonic tasted great.

"You're really enjoying that drink, aren't you, Tel?" Margaret said.

I nodded, and she squeezed my hand. "Good."

About an hour later up came a nice meal followed by coffee; that was all cleared away, the duty free trolley came round, and about half an hour after, the seatbelt and the no-smoking sign came on. The plane started its descent; it was a very smooth landing. Margaret leant over to me, kissed me, and said "Welcome to Malta."

After being checked through customs, we came out to the main airport area. There were a few people holding up names, and one chap was holding up "Terry and Margaret Parker." My friend John was on the ball; he said there would be a taxi waiting when I phoned him to tell him the dates. We jumped into his taxi, and off we went. The driver was chatting away in very good English, and we soon arrived at the flat.

As the driver drove off, a lady came across from a little bar opposite, and said, "Hi, you're Margaret and Terry."

"Yes, I said, "and you're English." We all laughed, and she opened the flat door, gave me the keys, and said, "When you have settled in, come over to the bar, have a drink, and I will tell you the lay of the land.

It was a first-floor flat of a two-floor apartment. It was very big, two bedrooms, toilet, a large bath and shower room, a kitchen, a large dinner/lounge, and the bonus – a large flat roof with sun beds. Margaret was very quiet. "You alright, my love?" I asked.

"Oh, Tel, it's marvellous. I just can't believe it." We were up on the roof, looking all round. The flat was on the edge of a large residential village. It was just perfect for us – no tourists, so we could eat and drink with the locals. Margaret was still quiet. "Come here and give me a kiss," I said.

"Tel, I'm so happy."

"Give us a kiss, then." She did, with great passion. "And again," I said, and Margaret obliged. "Come then, let's get unpacked and go over the road and have a drink."

We quickly unpacked. I put my shaving gear in the bathroom, and when I came out, Margaret was lying on the bed. I looked down to her. She looked up at me and said, "Darling," and smiled.

We went to the little bar over the road, and the lady introduced us to her husband, who had been born in Malta. She was a London girl. We all had a good chat and drink. She gave us the lay of the land, where the little shop was, good eating places, and the like. Then after a couple of hours her husband gave us a lift to a little restaurant bar to eat. It was a typical workmen's place, so we went in and sat down. A great big bloke came over, and in good English, asked what we would like. "Couple of steaks please" Over the years, this guy became a very good friend to us.

I said to Margaret, "You seem very quiet darling."

"I'm OK. Everything is so lovely, and I'm so happy." I leant over and kissed her. The chap brought over two very large T-bones, put one in front of Margaret and the other at the side of her. He looked at me, winked, and said, "You'll be happier sitting next to your lady, as you won't have to lean over." We all laughed.

We finished our meal, and we could hardly move. The bill was only £6. including two bottles of wine. Off we went a little wobble. We decided to stop at another bar and buy a bottle of wine to take back and have a drink; after all, we were on holiday.

Time was getting on; it was nearly ten thirty. We found a little bar after we had walked about fifteen minutes, and in we went. The barman seemed a very nice chap. After we had finished our lagers, I went to the bar and asked if I could have a bottle of wine and a couple of lagers to take away. The chap said it was no problem. I was beginning to like this Malta place.

We got back to the flat, climbed the stairs, and sat down to get our breath back. "What a day," I said to my Margaret.

"Yes, darling, what a day. Let's go up on the roof with a drink before we go to bed."

"I'm for that," I said, "lager or wine?"

"Let's take the lager; put the wine in the fridge for later," Margaret said, smiling and winking. We went up on the roof; it was lovely to see all the lights. Best of all, it was so warm. I undid my shirt. Margaret slipped her hand inside and up my back. She looked at me and said,

"Tel, I love you so much, and I'm so happy." Then she gave me a long kiss and said, "You're not too tired are you?" I kissed her hard and said, "I think it's time for bed."

I woke up at eight; my Margaret was still sleeping quietly. After I got dressed, Margaret woke. "What are you doing, darling?" she asked.

"I'm going up the shop to get a bit of breakfast," I said.

"Tel," Margaret said, " come back to bed for breakfast."

"I would love to, but the bloke will be here soon with the car." I then leant over and kissed her.

"Ooh, Tel, that's lovely."

Off I went to the shop. There were two nice young ladies running the shop. I got some butter, cheese, coffee, and a loaf of their lovely crusty bread; it's called "Hobser." The wine was silly money – twelve pence a bottle – and I bought six bottles.

I went back to the flat. I went upstairs and called, "I'm back love." Margaret came walking in to the kitchen, still wet and towelling herself. She came over and gave me a kiss. She went into the bedroom, and I took her in a cup of coffee, a chunk of bread and some cheese.

"Thanks darling," she said, "but we could have a better breakfast." She gave me a very cheeky grin, and I replied, "I know, but the bloke will be here with the car soon."

"OK, we will have to have a nice supper, then." I looked at her lovingly and said, "A good supper."

She said, "I will look forward to that," and again gave me that cheeky grin. I looked at her and thought, *She is such a beautiful lady. What a lucky bloke I am to have a lady like this, and how wonderful it is to be so in love with one another.*

Margaret looked at me and said, "You alright?"

"Yes," I said, "I was just thinking I was lucky to have such a lovely lady as you."

"No, Tel, I'm lucky to have you. You're a very kind, loving man. Also, Tel, you're my life." I went over to her cuddled her, and the towel fell to the floor. "What about the man who is bringing the car?"

"He will have to wait," I said.

A little later, we got dressed. Our coffee had gotten cold, so, as we were on holiday, we had a small glass of wine. We were halfway through drinking our wine when the bell went.

I went down and opened the door. It was the chap who'd picked us up at the airport. "Come up," I said.

"Are you settling OK?" he asked.

"Yes, thanks."

"Did you go out last night?"

"Yes, we went to the bar over the road, had a couple of drinks, then the owner took us down to a bar restaurant, where we had two great big steaks."

He laughed. "Were there two big chaps serving, one with a very deep voice?"

"Yes," we both said.

"That bar is down at the end of Hamrun Main Street. We will pass it as we go back to my office. The two chaps are brothers, and the steaks are the biggest and best on the island."

"You can say that again," I said. We all laughed.

"Right, let's get down to business." We sorted out all the paperwork and the times of the flight back home. We grabbed our bag, which we had already packed with towels, sun cream, and such, and off we went. The chap said he would drive so I could watch out for markers and get my bearings. He also said, "Don't worry about what side of the road to drive. It's similar to England, but in Malta, they drive down the middle. Don't worry what's behind you; just watch what's in front."

We all laughed, but we saw that he was not joking. As we passed the bar, the chap said, "That's where you were last night."

We carried on for about five minutes, then he seemed to do a handbrake turn and parked outside a little office and got out. He said, "It's all yours. Have a nice holiday." I got out, keeping the door open for Margaret to get in, then went round to the driver's side and got in.

"You OK, Tel?" Margaret said.

"Yes, I think so." I checked the gear stick, put her in gear, and drove off towards the way we came. "I think we will go into the bar we had our meal in last night to ask that big bloke the best places to go and where we can get a map."

"Good thinking, Batman," she said.

I found my way back quite easily and managed to park right outside of the bar. When we went into the bar, we were greeted by the big guy with the deep voice. "Good morning, lovebirds. How are you this morning?" He came over to us.

"Good morning," we replied. He then told us his name and asked us ours, saying that he couldn't keep calling us the lovebirds although he could see we were. "My name is Terry, and my lovebird, as you put it, is my lovely Margaret."

"That's Margarita here in Malta," he said. We carried on chatting, and he told us he went over to London to see his friend in the East End and was a Manchester United supporter. As he was talking, his brother brought over small little plates of nibbles, butter beans in olive oil, little bits of meat, bread with goats cheese, and what they call "baboosh" (small snails in their shells), which we both loved.

I ordered another two beers and asked where I could get a map also a safe place where we could go for a swim. Margaret couldn't swim yet, but I would teach her. He said there was a shop a few yards along where I could get a map, and he gave us directions to a little place where the water is shallow.

We walked along the street and just as he said, found a shop with cards on a stand outside, the shop was like one of our hardware shops. Margaret said, "Let's have a look round before you buy a map." We wandered inside; they seemed to sell everything.

"It would be a good idea if we could get one of those little fold-up cold bags and freeze blocks to carry wine in, if they sell them," Margaret said. They did, so I took one over to the counter with some blocks, and Margaret brought over a couple of small plastic cups and plastic containers with lids. "These will be handy," she said.

I then asked the lady behind the counter if she had a map of Malta, and the lady showed us several. One had a book attached showing things of interest. Margaret pointed to that one, and the lady put everything in a bag. We went back to the car and looked at the map to find where we were, and then we found the little bay the big guy had suggested.

I said to Margaret, "I have got to turn the car round first."

"No, you haven't," she said. "You have got to give me a kiss first." We had a couple of kisses then pulled off. After a couple of wrong turns, we finally found the little bay. It was a shallow entrance to the sea, and it was just a little step down onto a small sandy beach. There was a shop and a little bar; it seemed just perfect.

We changed into our swimwear in the car and went down to the water's edge. It was lovely and warm. Margaret walked in up to her waist with me alongside her, then I dropped down and had a little swim round. Then I came back to her, gave her a kiss, and said, "Right, let's get you swimming." Margaret dropped down, and with me holding her, she leant forward, did a couple of strokes, and then stood up. "Well done," I said and gave her another kiss (this one lasted longer).

We got out, towelled ourselves off, and went to the bar for a drink and something to eat. I got a bottle of wine, a couple of glasses, and a couple of mortadella-filled rolls. We sat there eating, drinking, and chatting like a couple of kids in love. After we had finished, we found a quiet place, put down our towels, lay in the lovely sun, and fell asleep. We woke up about two hours later. The sun was behind the hotel and we were in the shade. We looked at one another and knew that if the sun hadn't gone behind the hotel, we would have possible been badly sunburnt.

Back in the flat, we were soon on the roof with the cold wine, having a kiss and cuddle. We both had another glass of wine, and half a hour later we went down to get ready to go out. I asked Margaret, "Do you want to shower first?"

Margaret replied, "It's a big shower." I went into the shower and Margaret soon followed. (Well, you do need someone to wash your back for you.) We were in the shower for some time.

After towelling off and getting dressed, took some bottles back to the little shop and got six more and some supplies. The two very helpful young ladies who served in the shop advised us that the bread comes in first thing every morning and it's best to have it fresh. When we got back to the flat, we put the supplies in the fridge.

Margaret then asked, "Where are we going to eat tonight?" She knew how much I loved steak, but she couldn't handle another one.

I said we would park up in the main street, then we'd have a look at the different places.

"Sounds good to me, but we don't want to get back too late tonight," she said and winked. I pulled her over to me and kissed her. "Later," Margaret said, "otherwise, we won't get out." And she gave me a quick peck.

I parked up we got out and walked along, holding hands, chatting, and looking in the shops. We looked for a bar where we could eat. We found one that looked good, so in we went. It was quite big inside. The spaghetti looked good, so we ordered two and a bottle of wine; it was delicious, so good we that had another bottle. As we were drinking this, the owner came over, sat, and had a chat. As we left, Margaret said, "It's nice when they come over and have a chat with you." I agreed.

We got back to the flat, and I took off my shirt and said, "It's still very hot."

Margaret put the fan on in the bedroom and said, "Yes, it is." She took off her blouse and bra. "I think I will leave off my bra tomorrow, as I have noticed that a lot of ladies don't wear their bras. If you don't mind."

"I don't mind," I said, smiling.

Margaret looked at me and said, "I won't need any support." Then she paused and said," I don't know, though." We both laughed.

"Shall we go up on the roof and have a nightcap?" I said.

"Yes, OK," she said, and she put on her blouse.

"You go up and I will bring up the wine."

I gave Margaret her wine, said cheers, and we both sipped and put our glasses down on a little table. Margaret snuggled up to me, crying, and said, "I'm so happy."

"If you're happy, why are you crying?"

"Because I'm happy, Tel."

I turned to her, pulling her close. Her blouse was open, and I felt her breasts pushing hard to my chest. I kissed her hard, and she pulled me tight to her and kissed me back just as hard. "We deserve to be happy; we both have had some very bad times in the past."

"Shhh," she said and kissed me again. We broke away but kept our arms round each other's waist. When our drinks had gone, Margaret squeezed me tight and said, "Let's go down to bed."

I nodded. Margaret went straight to the bedroom. I went and got two more wines, took off the rest of my clothes, slid into bed, and cuddled up to Margaret. She smelt lovely and her body was soft. She had been right: "Sun, wine, and more love under a sheet."

The rest of the holiday went much the same. We packed in more in one week than others would in two, visiting the Silent City, the main big cities, ancient ruins, illegal drag car racing, churches, and many bars. We also made many friends. It was just a wonderful time, but most important, we were together for seven days and more in love than ever.

We got back home bubbling and telling Ralph all about it. We must have bored him, but we didn't care. We knew we must get our feet back on the ground; it was now getting late, so we all went to bed. The following morning was a typical Friday – raining. We had left all those lovely sunny skies behind. I quietly slipped out of bed without disturbing Margaret and went down to make some coffee. Ralph had already gone to work. I made a couple of cups and went upstairs into the bedroom. Margaret was still asleep. I put down the coffee then kissed Margaret and said, "Coffee, darling?" She opened her eyes and said, "No – you." I laughed and gave her another kiss, then leant over to get her coffee. She grabbed me before I could reach it and said, "You're teasing me," pulling me down for another kiss.

Later I had to go down and make another two coffees, as the first two had gone cold.

Later that morning I said to Margaret, as she was putting on the washing, "Fancy coming for a ride over to my flat? I want to check the answerphone also pick up the mail."

"OK, give me about ten minutes."

I parked right outside the flat, and we both went up. There were several calls, so I sorted them out first while Margaret opened the mail for me. None of the messages on the answering machine were urgent, so I made appointments for the following week. They sounded like good enquiries. The mail was mostly bills and a couple of cheques. There was also a letter from my solicitor, saying that if I admitted adultery and agreed to the terms enclosed, I wouldn't have to go to court and that it wouldn't cost too much. There were also some suggestions attached that he recommended. We put everything in a large envelope and locked and left the flat. I went to the little café just along the road and got a couple of rolls for lunch, then we drove back home.

When we got in, Margaret said "You go and make some coffee, love." I will get on with all this paperwork."

I brought in the coffee, and Margaret was typing away. I just don't know how I got on without her. I said, "How about taking five to have your coffee and rolls?"

"I will just finish this invoice," she said. She stopped typing about five minutes later, sat next to me, and started to sip at her coffee.

"I think I will go on what the solicitor has laid out in his draft. If I start changing things or asking for things, it's going to get nasty and drag on."

"Tel, I feel so sorry for you. You're going to lose everything you have worked for."

"No, I won't," I said. "I will have you." She pulled me over and gave me a big kiss. "Shall I say that again?" I asked.

She smiled. "You'll say anything for a kiss."

I nodded. "Now I want to have a serious chat with you, love," I said.

"Here we go again, the Birmingham restaurant." We both laughed.

"No, listen. There are two things. First, I will put the word round and start looking round for a little lock-up shop round this area to turn into a studio, and second – now this is a very big decision for you to make, very big – would you leave the design council and come with me as my partner in the company?"

Margaret looked at me with those big brown eyes. *God, she is a beautiful lady,* I thought.

"Tel," she said, "you're right; it's a very big decision to make. Looking at your workload, it's doubled since I have been doing the books. The gamble is will it carry on improving? Tel, I have a lot of faith in you. Also, I know you work very hard, and of course, I love you very much. So yes, I will, but we will have to get somewhere as a studio-office first."

I grabbed her and kissed her hard. "Hang on," she said, "you don't want to break my ribs!"

"Sorry, darling. I'm so happy."

Three weeks later, our local greengrocer told us he had heard there was a little shop opposite him going up for rent. He gave us the agent's name, for there was no board up yet advertising it. So I rang the agent and made an appointment to see him at the shop that evening.

It was about 400 yards from Margaret's house. It was on a corner. Through the front door was a big area with windows both sides –plenty of light. Then, through a little lobby, was a back room with a kitchen and, at the other end of the room, a door through to a little toilet.

"It looks good," I said, and Margaret nodded. We came back into the front room, and the agent then said, "That flap door that you're standing on leads to the cellar."

I opened it and went down a wobbly old staircase, switched on the light, and was well pleased. It was quite a big area. I could store clients' displays, and it would help to pay the rent, but I would have to put in a new staircase and a bigger flap. I turned off the light and came up.

Looking at the agent, I asked the rent. After he told us, I asked Margaret what she thought. "Seems OK," she said, "bearing in mind what you are paying now, including parking and petrol."

Together we looked at the agent and said, "We'll take it."

"Good," he said. "Give me your evening phone number, and I will give you a ring to see you both with the rent book, keys, and of course I will need a cheque for the first month's rent."

When we got indoors, I poured out a couple of wines to celebrate and said I would have to find a second-hand office furniture shop.

"That's my department," Margaret quickly said, "for at the council, they are always throwing out furniture when it's replaced by new furniture. I will speak to the chap who stores it all, ready to be collected, and see what they have got."

"Great," I said. "You're a doll." Then I told her about my idea of storing clients' displays in the cellar to help with the rent.

"What a good idea," she said, "but what about that wobbly old staircase?"

"Don't worry; I will make a new one. Once I get the keys I can go in and measure it up, and then I can get my contractor to make it in sections for me. I'll also check the whole area size and get some carpet off the chaps who do my stands for me."

"Now you're cooking, baby," Margaret said. "You're beginning to think like proper businessman now, not like an out-of-work artist."

I went to the flat the following morning and got a couple of rolls from the café as usual. There were a couple of messages on the answer machine, a new contact and a client who want me to look after and run the office and drawing exhibition in Manchester that I had designed some months ago.

I finished a design I had been doing for a German electric appliance company then rang the client about the job in Manchester. He was out so I said I would ring tomorrow, but I asked the lady I was talking to what date the exhibition was. It would be in six weeks' time. I sat there for a moment, thinking about Margaret leaving her job, the new studio, and this thing in Manchester. I was worried about my Margaret packing up her job and what would happen if it all went wrong. *I love that lady. I just can't hurt her. Are we doing the right thing?* Then I thought, *I have been there before, with my back against the wall, and come out fighting; the difference this time is I have help from a lovely, intelligent lady, who has given me a lot of confidence and a lot of love. I will talk it over with her tonight.*

I got back on the drawing board, tarted up the German job, ready to get the dyeline prints done, then rang the new contact. This made me sit up and listen; it was a very big Japanese toy company who would like to see me regarding submitting a design for their stand in next year's toy fair. I made an appointment to see them the following week. *If I get this, what I was worried about would start to fade away. With the other toy companies' stands that I do, it would be a great start for a new year. God I could do with a gin now.* But I had another coffee, thinking, *I'm a good boy.*

I left early to take the dyelines to the printer and said I would pick them up tomorrow morning. I got to Margaret's street just as the pub opened. Gasping, I went in and had a half of lager.

"No gin?" the landlord said.

"No," I said, "I'm trying to take things easy for a bit."

"I don't blame you," he said, "as it can become a problem to some." After about twenty minutes, I left, went round to the off-licence, and got a couple of bottles of wine. I drove back to Margaret's house to wait, but up came Ralph from work. He let me in after the usual thump, and I flopped on the couch.

"You look tired," Ralph said.

"Yeah, I am. Had a long day."

"Don't worry, Mum will be here soon," he said.

I put the telly on, and Ralph went up to his room. I soon heard his record player going, and ten minutes later Margaret came in.

"Hallo, darling," she said, giving me a quick peck. "Just going to put the dinner on, then I want to have a talk to you." She went into the kitchen, and I thought, *That sounds funny; I haven't done anything wrong – or have I?*

In came Margaret and sat down.

"Would you like a drink?" I asked.

"Not at the moment," Margaret said. "Now, Tel, what's the problem?"

"Margaret, I'm worried that if you leave your job—"

"Stop, Tel. Don't worry, I know it will work. You're a good designer; you just need a bit more confidence. Now, regarding me leaving my job," she laughed and said, "I have already put in a months' notice. Are you alright now?" I nodded. "Then give us a kiss, and I will have a glass of wine now."

I then told Margaret about the new inquiry from the big toy company.

"That's good; I told you not to worry," she said. "I'm going to check on the dinner." As Margaret got into the kitchen, the phone went. "Answer, please, love," she shouted.

I picked up the phone, and it was the agent for the shop, "Sorry to ring you so late, but I know you would like to move in ASAP, so can you meet me there about five tomorrow evening?"

"No problem," I said. "See you then." I went into the kitchen and told Margaret. Then I said I had forgotten to tell her about the Manchester exhibition date. "Don't worry. Tell me after dinner, as its ready. Would you give Ralph a shout?" I did, and he came down the stairs like a herd of elephants.

After dinner, we went back into the front room. I poured some more wine and sat down. I looked at Margaret and said, "Now this exhibition in Manchester that I told you about, it's in six weeks' time, and we will have to be there from Monday till Friday or Saturday for the build up and pull out and run the show when it's open, staying in the hotel."

"What do you mean by running it?" Margaret asked.

"Man reception and get visitors to sign in, make sure that the buffet is always good, and keep the exhibitors happy."

"That sounds OK, but also, we could do a bit of business. You never know, we could pick up some work for the future."

"You're a little darling," I said.

"Well, what about a reward then?" she said. I leant over and kissed her. "Is that all I get?"

"At the moment," I replied.

"I see – playing hard to get." We both laughed.

The following day I left the flat early after getting the outstanding work done. I got to the shop early, and I was pleased I had, as the agent also arrived early. We went in the shop and sorted out the paperwork. After he left, I went to the car, got a tape and pad, went back in, and started to measure up for the carpet. After that, I lifted up the flap and wrote down the sizes and made a rough drawing of a staircase. I looked at the flap. I would have to get a bigger one made, so I worked out the size and how I could fit it. It was possible I would need a bit of help in fitting it, so I thought I would ask Ralph when I got home.

When I got in, Margaret was in the kitchen making dinner, and Ralph was upstairs playing his records. Margaret said, "I drove round the top way and saw your car outside the shop; how did you get on?"

"OK. I got all the measurements I need. I will draw up the staircase and the size of a block board flap tomorrow. Then I'll post it to the contractor and ask them how soon they could have it done. Also, I will ring my mate for a van the day after next to pick up the furniture from the design council. The greengrocer's son said he would help unload."

The following day I was at the flat early. That afternoon, I picked up the van, collected the furniture, and took it back to the shop. The lad over the road helped me of load, and I gave him a fiver. He was well pleased. I took the van back and went in my mate Chas's office to settle up. After, I sat with him and had a cup of coffee. He looked at me and said, "Tel, you look knackered."

"Yes," I said, "I have been doing a lot lately."

"Why don't you and your lady go on one of these bargain-break weekends? They are very cheap. Look, I have details here of the Grand Hotel in Brighton. I looked at it; it seemed like a good deal – £26 bed, breakfast, and evening meal, with live music Saturday night. Two nights, go for it," my mate said. "You love this lady so much, you tell me, so treat her."

"OK," I said, "give me your phone." I rang the Grand and booked the weekend under the name of Mr and Mrs Parker.

"Well done, Tel. It will do you good," he said. "Now don't forget, I'm going in the chair of my lodge in six weeks' time, and you're invited."

"OK, yes," I said, still thinking about the weekend at the Grand. I left with my head buzzing.

Margaret was already home when I arrived. "You're early," I said.

"Not really," she replied and gave me a kiss. I looked at my watch. It was later than I'd thought. I poured a couple of wines and took them in the kitchen. I passed one to Margaret, and she looked at me and said "Thanks. Now out with it."

"Out with what?" I asked I pulled her over and kissed her.

"You can't get round me like that. What is it; have you been a naughty boy?" she said.

I laughed. "I'm always a good boy, as you know, but I have booked a bargain break for the weekend so we can have a well-earned rest."

She cuddled up to me and said, "If they have a big bed, it won't be a rest." She kissed me on the neck. "Where are we going?"

"Get your best knickers on, my love. It's the Grand at Brighton."

"Bloody hell, Tel, two pair of knickers."

"Till I get you to the bedroom," I said.

"You're getting cheeky just because you think that in a posh hotel you will get your wicked ways," she said.

"Won't I?" I replied.

"I will need persuading."

"No problem," I said.

"OK, let's go up and try out your persuading talents, then."

"Who am I to argue?" So up we went to bed.

After a few days, I went and took the brief from the new client for their stand in the toy fair, rang my carpet contractor to tell him I needed some carpet, and rang my solicitor to tell him to go ahead with the divorce as his draft. He said he would send me a letter to sign and return. I looked at my watch I had a hour to kill before I left, it was too late to start working out a design for the new toy company, so I thought I had better ring my mum and dad and get all the flack they were going to throw over with.

My mother answered the phone. "Hallo, Mum," I said.

"Hallo, boy," Mum answered. I thought that was good; if she was going to have a go, she would have called me Terry.

"How are you both?" I inquired.

"Fine, but a bit fed up with the weather. What about you and your lady?"

"I'm fine and the happiest I have ever been in my life," I said.

I told Mum and Dad about Margaret and that she would be quitting the design council to work with me. I also said that the divorce was going through and that I would marry Margaret one day.

Then my dad said, "When are we going to see Margaret?"

"I will try to bring her down to see you in a couple of weeks' time."

"OK, we will make her very welcome."

"Thank you, Dad. It will mean a lot to me."

I got to Margaret's later than usual, as there was a lot of traffic about. Margaret was at the door. "You alright, Tel? You're late," she said.

I kissed her and said, "Don't worry; be happy," using one of her sayings.

"You find your own sayings," was her giggling answer.

After we had eaten, I said to her, "Are you still looking forward to going to the Grand?"

"I'm very excited," she answered. "Have you ever stayed there before?"

"Yes, a couple of times, when the toy fair used to be at Brighton."

"What's it like?"

"You'll love it, and it will love you."

"What do you mean, Tel?"

"Margaret, you're a lady who demands respect with your presence, so you will walk in there admired."

"Tel, you have rose-coloured spectacles, but I'm very proud that you treat me like this. I'm so happy to be loved so much by you; we are so lucky to have this love."

"Stop that crying now," I said.

"Sorry, Tel, I'm so happy." We then embraced.

"Right, my love, while you're in a happy mood—"

"What you up to now?" she said, looking at me with those great big brown eyes, which were slightly tearful.

"I spoke to my mum and dad, and they would very much like to meet you."

"Yes, it's about time I met them, so they can see what a wicked woman their son has fallen in love with." She giggled.

"I will make no comment," I said.

"I didn't think you would," Margaret answered and giggled again.

"What's all this giggling about?"

"I don't know. It could be happiness, love, wine, or all of these – I don't know." She giggled again.

"I'm getting no sense out of you at the moment," I said.

"I don't care; give us a kiss, then," she said.

"Margaret, you're such a lovely lady, and when you're in this mood you're not just a lovely lady, but you're so funny."

"You're taking the Mick out of me, Tel," she said, giggling again.

"No, darling, I just love you. It's lovely to see you so happy and bubbly."

She came over to me, put her arms round my neck, looked up at me, and said, "Oh, Tel," then kissed me hard and passionate. Then she said, "Tel, let's go to bed." I kissed her back with every ounce in my body. Then I took her hand and went up to bed knowing this lovely lady was my life.

The following morning, Margaret snuggled up to me. "I would like to stay here all day with you," she said.

"So would I, but work has to be done."

"Just one more cuddle, please, Tel."

"Alright, but that's all."

"Spoilsport," she said, giggling. We got up about half an hour later. I told her that she would be late. "I don't care, I'm leaving," she replied and giggled.

"You're at it again; have you got ants in your knickers?"

"I haven't got any on yet," she replied, giggling again.

I went over to her and kissed her. "I'll see you tonight."

"OK, love, about six," she said.

I had a bad drive again, a lot of traffic, but I finally got to the flat, parked the car, and up I went. I put the kettle on and listened to the answer machine. I had two messages from old clients wanting to see me later. The post was not really interesting, except for a nice large cheque. After I got a couple of rolls, I started drawing up the new toy company's stand that I had roughed out earlier. I worked late in the afternoon eating the rolls and drinking about a dozen cups of coffee, thinking, *I'm not drinking gin now but addicted to bloody coffee.*

It was a good drive to Margaret's, not a lot of traffic. *That makes a change,* I thought. The door was open so in I went. "Hallo, darling," Margaret said and gave me a kiss.

"Hallo, love," I said as I kissed her back.

"I knew you wouldn't be long; I saw the car outside the off-licence." I put the bottles I'd just gotten in the fridge and took one out that was already in there. I poured two glasses and gave one to Margaret. Then I asked her if she could get home by three tomorrow.

"Why, where are we going?" she asked, teasing. "Yes, I can leave the council round lunchtime."

"By the way, we got a nice cheque today. I have brought it over for you to enter.

"OK, I will do it after our evening meal."

"There is something I forgot to say last night, with you larking about. I would like to take you down and meet my mum and dad next weekend, if it's OK with you."

"Yes, love, I have got to meet them someday. When will we go, Friday or Saturday?"

"I don't know yet, I will have to check with them. But I must warn you, Dad makes his own wine, and it's lethal."

"Then we will have to go to bed early then." She winked.

"You behave."

"If I did you wouldn't love me," she said and started to giggle again.

After dinner Margaret told Ralph that all his dinners would ready in the fridge for the weekend; all he had to do was heat them up. "Mum," he said, "don't worry. I can look after myself. You and Tel have a good time; you both deserve it. I know you have had a lot of problems, Tel. But you love my mum so much it makes me very happy."

"Ralph, that's a really nice thing to say."

"It's OK, Tel," he answered. I looked across at Margaret and could see she was well moved, so I just got up went over to her and put my arm round her then gave her a squeeze. She looked at me with watering eyes and for the first time, didn't say anything.

Ralph got up and said he was going round to his mates. As soon as he went out, Margaret burst out crying. "That was so lovely, Tel. I knew he was very fond of you, but I didn't know it was that much." I just cuddled her. There wasn't much I could say. When she stopped crying, I asked if she would like another glass of wine. "Yes, please. I really need one now after that." I gave her another glass, and she sipped it then looked at me with her big watering eyes. I pulled her towards me and kissed her gently. "Thank you," she said.

The following morning Margaret was still very excited that we were going to the Grand. "I have never been to Brighton before, and the Grand, that's a real treat. I had better get a nightie."

"What for, to put under the pillow in case of fire?" I laughed.

"Behave, Tel."

"If I did, you wouldn't love me," I replied."I will see you later."

"OK, love, hang on a minute." She went to her bag. "Here, I forgot to give it to you last night, it's the front door key. I had it cut yesterday."

"Thanks, darling," I said and gave her a quick peck on the cheek.

"Is that all I get?" she asked, giggling again.

"Yes, at the moment. Later will be different."

"OK, I will let you off then."

I parked outside the flat, got a couple of rolls as usual, and went up. There were no messages, but there were a couple of letters: one from my solicitor, which I needed to sign so he could proceed with the divorce, and another cheque. *Great! Since Margaret has been doing the books, cheques seem to come in sooner.* I sipped at my coffee and started to munch at one of the rolls.

The phone went; it was my contractor, saying the stairs and flap were ready and one of his vans was going to Olympia next Tuesday. He said he would drop it off then, about eight in the morning. *If I can get that made up and fitted in the next week or so, then get the carpet all laid before we go to Manchester, we could move in when we come back. Now I'm getting a bit excited.*

I finished the second roll then rang my mum and dad. My mum answered. "Hallo, Mum."

"Hallo, boy, you alright?"

"Yeah, not too bad," I said. "I would like to bring Margaret down next weekend, if that's OK."

"We would love to see you and meet Margaret, what does she eat?" Typical Mum, thinking of grub.

"Mum, my Margaret eats anything," I said, hearing dad shouting in the background.

"Boy, Dad wants to know if your lady drinks wine."

"You tell Dad my lady, as he puts it, likes wine, and she loves your son. Her name is Margaret, not 'my lady', as I haven't been knighted, yet."

"OK, boy, you let me know roughly what day and time next week."

"OK, Mum, bye for now."

Right, I thought, *what else is there to do? Yes, let the chap in charge of the minicab office know I won't be there the weekend. No, on second thought, I won't say the flat will be empty.* I was just going to leave, and the phone went. It was my carpet contractor; he said he would have a big piece of dark brown carpet and could drop it in the shop about eight Thursday night. "That would be smashing," I said. *Wait till I tell my Margaret all this good news – and the cheque as a bonus. What a good weekend we are going to have!*

When I got to Margaret's house, she was already there. I let myself in. "That you, Tel?" she shouted from upstairs.

"No, it's your fancy man," I teased.

"Shut up," was the reply. I went upstairs and told her all the news and about getting the cheque. "Good, I will enter the cheque in the books before we go. Then you can post it on the way."

I went over to her and put my arm round her waist. "Did you get the nightie, darling?" I asked. She turned and looked at me with those big brown eyes and said with a very cheeky smile, "No, but I got another bottle of Calvin Klein." I tried to kiss her, but she giggled again. "It's my turn to play hard to get."

I just looked at her and said, "You're lovely."

"Tel, start packing or we will never get there. You want to get in front of the Friday traffic."

"OK, love, you're right." I started to pack, then added, "Don't forget to put in an evening dress."

"I have packed two, so you can tell me which one you like best." She then asked me to take her case down when I was ready, as she wanted to go down and enter the cheque in the books.

Twenty minutes later, we were on the road. We stopped just round the corner to post the cheque, then we were off again; we had a fair drive down, getting to the Grand just before six. My Margaret was bubbling.

I parked the car right outside, and a porter came out and got the cases. We followed him to reception and were greeted by the lady there. I said, "I have a room booked – Mr and Mrs Parker." She looked at her book, told me our room number, and gave me the key. I thanked her and asked if the bar was open.

"Yes, sir," she replied. "I will get the porter to take your cases up to your room."

Margaret got hold of my hand as we walked towards the bar. "What drink are you going to get, Mrs Parker?" She asked, and she started to giggle. "I couldn't book in as Mr Parker and Margaret, could I?" She squeezed my hand and giggled again.

We had a great time. Margaret looked a million dollars in an evening dress and my dancing lessons came in handy, but Margaret…

well, could that lady dance! After, she told me that she had many medals for ballroom and Latin, and I could well believe it.

On the way home, Margaret said, "Can we go there again? It was lovely." And we did, many times on bargain breaks, also two Christmases, and got to know the manager and staff very well. One time on a bargain break I remember well, we went to the grand to celebrate my divorce and had a great Saturday night, at breakfast, Margaret ask if we could have a Buck's fizz? Why not I said and called over the waiter, "did you want glasses or a bottle of champagne and a jug of orange juice?" "the bottle please" I answered, a couple of minutes up he came with the jug, bottle and a couple of glasses, he got quite a few looks from some of the guests, "would you like me to open it now sir" "yes please" I said, now when the champagne was opened there was a very loud pop, everyone looked round, and Margaret said in a loud voice, "Good night, darling" the waiter nearly dropped the bottle, I nearly choked on a mouthful of breakfast, a couple of ladies giggled, some just looked and most of the chaps looked down frighten to laugh and Margaret just carried on eating her breakfast, I can tell you it was hilarious, as we came out of the restaurant the waiter said to Margaret "you have made my day, I will remember that for a long time" Margaret laughed and said "It's all good fun also it woke some of the old stodgers up and I'm wicked"

We arrived home about lunchtime, so we popped down the pub at the bottom of the road to have a drink and get some shellfish for our evening meal off the stall outside. My Margaret was still bubbling about the great time we had, so I said that when we weren't working at the weekends, we could always go to hotels in the country to recharge ourselves, "I would love that, Tel. You feel so good after…"

"After what?" I said.

"Behave yourself," she whispered.

We wandered home, chatting and larking about all the way like a couple of kids. We got in and started talking about our programme for the following week. When the exhibition in Manchester was finished, I would pre-book a self-drive van and move all my stuff from the flat to the new shop on Saturday. Then we would have that Sunday to sort everything out.

"That sounds good to me," Margaret said. "Have I done a sign with the company's name to be fixed outside?"

I looked at her and feebly said no.

"Typical. You do everything for others but forget yourself."

"Sorry, I will sort it out tomorrow," I said.

"OK, I will let you off if you give me a kiss."

"Only a kiss?"

"Well I'm open to offers." She started to giggle again.

"What am I going to do with you?" I said.

"What you like darling. Let's have an early night."

"I can do with a rest."

"Yes, you need a rest my love," she said, and winking.

The following week was a mixture of work at the flat and the shop. I ordered a board from my contractor so I could write our company's name on it. Margaret said I should stop calling it the shop and call it our studio, and I agreed. I got onto my insurance firm, and I transferred all my equipment to the new studio in Blythe road when we came back from the Manchester show.

In the middle of the week I rang my mum and dad to check if everything was OK for Friday. It was, so I told my Margaret it was still on, but I know she was very nervous about meeting them. "OK," she said, "I will finish at lunchtime on Friday so we can get away early."

Friday at two thirty, I rang mum and said we were on our way. We were making good time, until I said, "Only about 10 miles to go."

A couple of minutes later, she asked me to stop. We had just passed a lay-by sign so we were soon at it. I pulled in, and before I could say anything, Margaret was out and being sick.

I got out and ran round to her. "What's the matter love?"

"I'm so worried, Tel."

"Don't. It will be alright. They understand what's happened, really."

"I will be OK in a minute," she said. After she got in the car, we sat for a while, then Margaret said she was OK, so I started the car and off we went.

On arriving at Mum and Dad's bungalow, I asked Margaret if she was OK. "My tummy is spinning," she replied. I told her not to worry, things would be OK, and she smiled and nodded, but I could see she was still worried. I got out of the car went round to open Margaret's door, and as I did, I heard my dad shout out, "Have a good run down, boy?" He was at the front door.

"Yeah, not too bad. This is my Margaret." Dad put both hands on her shoulders, kissed her on the cheek, and said, "Lovely to meet my lad's lady." Then he looked at me and nodded. The first part was over, and Margaret seemed to relax a bit.

We went into the hall where Mum was waiting. "Hi, Mum. This is my Margaret." Mum took hold of her hand, kissed her on the cheek, and said, "Nice to meet you."

We all went into the lounge, and as we sat down, Dad said, "I bet you could do with a drink now after that drive."

"Not arf," I said, looking at Margaret.

Dad said, "Would you like a glass of wine, Margaret?"

"Please," she answered.

"What about me?" I asked.

"You can wait. Ladies first." He gave all but Mum a large glass then said cheers.

Margaret asked, "What about your wife?"

Mum said, "I don't drink, Margaret, and you can just call me Mum."

We sat chatting and drinking wine, then dad asked Margaret if she would like to see what he was growing in his greenhouse. They went into the garden, and Mum looked at me and said, "Me and your dad knew this would happen one day, but it comes as a shock. But your lady is a very intelligent, lovely lady, and I can see you love one another very much. Also, I shouldn't say this, but I can see in your eyes a lot more than what you ever had before. I hope and pray you will be very happy. Looking at you both, I'm sure you will, as there is a bond you have that is never seen nowadays. God bless you, boy. It's so lovely to see you happy." Mum then came over and kissed me on the cheek.

Dad came back in with Margaret; they were laughing together. Dad said, "This lady knows a lot about flowers and plants."

"She also knows how to make your son happy," I said, then I thought, *God I wish I hadn't said that.* But Margaret was quick and jumped in and said, "Yes, I do all the invoices, paperwork, and costing, leaving Tel to concentrate on his drawings."

"That's good," Mum said, "as he is useless at paperwork." We all laughed.

"Let's have some more wine before we go in for dinner, as I have a different blend I would like you try at dinner," Dad said.

"Him and his bloody wine, that's all he thinks of," Mum said.

I said, "I'm not complaining."

"What about poor Margaret having to keep drinking his wine?"

"Fifth amendment," I said, and Margaret giggled.

I asked Mum where we would be sleeping, as I wanted to unpack.

"In our room," she answered.

As Margaret and I were unpacking in my mum and dad's bedroom, I said, "This is a bit of a surprise."

Margaret nodded and said, "I think they like me. Also, your dad's a bit of a lad. I can see where you get it from." She laughed.

"Maybe, but I know that I'm a lot kinder."

"I will go along with that," she said. I gave her a quick cuddle and kiss then we went back to the lounge.

"All OK?" Mum said.

"Yes, and thanks for leaving the empty drawer for us."

Mum then said, "I must go and get the dinner ready."

"I will come and give you a hand," Margaret said and followed her out.

I looked at Dad and said, "What do you think?"

"She's a very nice lady, boy, and you seem to act as one. She's not frightened of work, so together you are well suited. Now what's happening about your family?"

"The divorce is going through," I said, and as I did that, Mum shouted, "Dinner's ready."

"OK," I called back then said to Dad, "I will tell you all about it later."

After dinner, Margaret helped Mum to wash up. I sat in the lounge and told dad all about the divorce settlement. After I had finished, Dad said, "Well, boy, you know what you're doing, but you have lost everything you have worked so hard for in your life."

"I know, Dad, but I have never been so happy as I am now."

"I can see that, boy. You're a changed man. And meeting and talking to Margaret, I know she will help you in your job. Also, she thinks the world of you." He then put out his hand and said, "Good luck to you both, son. Me and Mum hope it will all work out. Looking at you two, I'm sure it will."

I was just going to thank him, but the ladies came back in. We all sat chatting and, of course, drinking more wine until just after ten. It had been a long drive, so Margaret and I went to bed a little boozy and very tired.

At eight the following morning, there was a knock on the door, and in came Dad with two coffees. He said good morning, put the cups on the bedside tables, and drew the curtains letting the sun to shine through the nets. As he left, he said breakfast would be about nine.

"OK," we said together. I looked at Margaret, gave her a quick kiss, and sat up to get my coffee.

"Is that all I get?" she laughingly said.

"You behave yourself," I answered.

"Why?" she asked, giggling again, then she pulled herself up to get her coffee.

After breakfast, Dad said we could have a run into Poole, have a look round the harbour, and on the way back, call in the British legion club for a drink. "Sounds good to us," I said, and Margaret agreed. Then she told them she used to be a wren at the same time I was in the army. "I piped in both, stationed at Portsmouth at the same time."

"What a coincidence," Mum said.

"I wish we had met then," I said, then I realised I had put my foot in it again.

Margaret again quickly came to my rescue and said, "How far is Poole harbour from here, Dad?"

Mum looked at me, and I thought, *She's not silly. She knows that Margaret is trying to cover up for what I said, as she didn't want to bring up things that happened in my early life.* Then Mum gave me a knowing smile.

The rest of the day went well; we went to the harbour, then to the club, back home for a bit of grub and of course more wine, then an early night. Margaret snuggled up to me in bed, gave me a lovely kiss, and said how much she had enjoyed her day.

At eight in the morning, there was a bang on the door. It was Dad on his coffee run. He said good morning, drew the curtains, and went out saying, "Breakfast at the usual time."

Margaret and I had a little laugh and cuddled up, waiting for our coffee to cool. Margaret felt so warm and soft that I wished we were home in our own bed. She gave me a little dig in the ribs and said, "Behave. I know what you're thinking."

"How?" I said.

"Because I'm thinking the same thing."

"Give us a kiss then," I said, "before we get up."

"What a good idea."

It was midday when we said our goodbyes. We said that we would pop down in a month or so; they wished us a safe journey and said to give them a ring when we got home.

"It wasn't too bad, was it?" I said to Margaret.

"No, they were very kind, and they know we are just not a five-minute wonder." We carried on chatting all the way home, and as soon as we got in, Margaret rang them to let them know we were home safe. I heard her laugh and say, "I will. Goodbye."

"What was that all about?" I asked.

"Your mum told me to look after you, and I said I would."

"OK then, give me a kiss and cuddle."

"I never thought you'd ask." We had a quick embrace and decided to go out to finish the weekend off, as Ralph's dinner was already in the fridge.

The following week was Margaret's last at the design council. I got the board for the sign, and my contractor had painted it white for me, so all I had to do was write it. I checked with the client I was doing the Manchester job for, to let him know that everything was OK and it would be delivered on Sunday early. We needed to have it all set up by midday Monday latest, then the exhibitors would have plenty of time to put up their displays.

I told Margaret that we would be going up to Manchester on the Saturday, and reminded her that I would be going to London by train in the middle of the week. "I'm in charge then," she said, laughing. Then she said they were having a little send-off party at the council on Friday; I was invited, and she would let me know the time tomorrow.

The following day was a bit hectic. I had five phone calls – three existing clients, all for graphic work, and two new clients, one for graphics and the other for a stand at the NEC. I had to finish and send off a coloured visual with block plan and elevation to a car-radio company and finish off my sign board for the new studio, for I didn't really want to work the following day with packing, sorting out my travelling display and sign-writing box, and Margaret's party, which I hoped would be in the afternoon.

I got to Margaret's just after six and let myself in. "Hallo, darling," she said, and she gave me a welcome kiss. "I poured out a couple of glasses of wine when I heard your car pull up."

"I didn't think we had any left. I was going to go round and get some once you knew I was home."

"I got a couple of bottles as I passed the shop."

"What a star."

"Yes, I know I am," she said, giggling.

"Modest, too," I said and took the glass off her. "Cheers."

I went into the kitchen while Margaret was doing the dinner. She looked at me and told me the party tomorrow would be about three.

"OK," I replied. "I will be there chatting up your Rosemary."

"Oh, so you fancy your chances?"

I just shrugged my shoulders and laughed.

When dinner was ready, Margaret asked me to give Ralph a shout. Again like a herd of elephants, he came charging down the stairs. "What-o, Tel," he said, giving me my usual thump, "how ya doing?"

"Not so bad," I said, thumping him on the shoulder.

"Pack it up, you two," Margaret said as she came out of the kitchen with a plate full of food. "One day, one of you is going to get hurt if you keep mucking about like that."

Friday came, and we both were up early. I got to the car park near the design council at ten to four, parked up, and walked round to the offices. That nice posh lady was still here. "Hallo again," she said. "You're taking our Margaret away from us, but we all know that you will look after her."

"Yes, I will look after her, and I will tell you a secret: one day I will marry her."

She laughed. "Yes, we all know that as well." She then picked up the phone, pressed the button, waited for a few seconds, and said, "Rosemary, Margaret's fiancé Terry is here."

Minutes later, the lift doors opened and out walked Rosemary. "Hallo, Terry. I bet you're a happy man today," she said as we got into the lift.

"I am now and have been the happiest man in the world for a long time now, as you well know."

She looked at me and laughed. "You have lost quite a bit of weight since I last saw you."

"Yes, I feel a lot better in losing it." With that, the lift doors opened and we walked along to the conference room. Margaret came straight over and gave me a kiss. Then she introduced me to the staff; she introduced me as her fiancé and working partner.

About half an hour later, her boss called order, asked Margaret to come over, and gave her a going-away gift. Before Margaret could thank him, he called me over and said, "We would all like to wish you success working together in the future, and we know you will stay as happy as you are now."

Back home, we both flopped in on the sofa. We looked at one another, and I said, "How ya doing, partner?" Margaret snuggled up to me and said, "I love you so much Tel," and she kissed me. I kissed her back and said "So do I, and now think – we will be together all the time, day and night, as we have dreamed for always."

"Oh, Tel, we will have a wonderful life together," she said, pulling me tighter to her.

"Yes," I said, and we kissed again.

We must have dozed off, for the next I remember was the front door closing and Ralph shouting, "Hi, Mum and Tel. I'm home." We went to bed early, as we had a long drive the following day; also, we wanted to enjoy the rest after a very emotional day for both of us.

We left early Saturday morning for Manchester and arrived at the hotel round about midday. After we unpacked quickly, we went down to the bar for a drink and snack. About an hour later, I asked the bar steward if he could contact the banquet manager for me. We had met before, so I introduced her to Margaret then asked if we could mark out the positions of the stands ahead of time, as the banquet room was empty. She said it would be no problem and left, at which point, Margaret said to me, "You have a way of chatting up ladies," and started to giggle.

"Is that the way I chatted you up?"

"No, you silly bugger, you just got me to fall in love with you." She leant over to me and gave me a kiss.

We finished our drinks, then went to the banquet room. I put on the lights, and Margaret said, "It's huge." I had to go up to the room and get the plans and my site box, and when I came back, I spread the drawing out on a table and started to line things up and measure out the areas. I called in the bar and got a couple of drinks to keep us going. Once we got the first one sorted, the rest just fell into place, but it still took up the rest of the afternoon. On finishing, we congratulated ourselves on a job well done. We finished our drinks and went up to our room

We were down to breakfast early so we would be ready when the van arrived. We both knew that unloading would take up quite some time, as the banquet room was two floors up from where the van could park and the quickest way to get the shell and displays up to the room was to use the fire stairs. This was the biggest pain doing shows in this hotel, especially if it's raining – and in Manchester, it's always raining.

We had just finished breakfast and were going to the banquet room when the receptionist came over to tell me the driver had arrived. He had come early. In ten minutes, the shell scheme was being bought into the room. With Margaret's help, we started to set up the modular shell. It was a light system and went together easy. By the time they had finished bringing up the shell, we had a third of it up. I told the lads to have a break before they started to bring up the exhibitors' equipment. Margaret ordered coffee and sarnies. After a half-hour break, we all started again. By the time they had all the exhibitors' equipment up, we had the shell up. Margaret got the drawings and showed the lads what stand the equipment had to be put at, as some of it was heavy. I sorted out the lighting, for once that was all done, the lads could go, just leaving me and my lovely assistant to put up the graphics. So far everything was going well.

The lads were finished about three. I offered them a drink, but they wanted to get off and said would stop when they got on the M1. I gave them £10 each to have a drink, and they thanked us both, adding, "See ya on the pull out," and off they went.

We carried on putting up the graphics till six, and I said "That's it for today, as we only have about an hour's work to do tomorrow."

Margaret said, "Good, then come over to me." She gave me a cuddle and said, "Didn't we do well?"

"Let's go, sit, and have a drink in the bar before we go up to shower and get ready for dinner."

"I never thought you'd ask," she said with a suggestive smile.

"I said a drink."

"Yes, you also said a shower." She giggled.

"Come on, let's have that drink," I answered.

We finally got to the bar, and I asked what her what she would like to drink. "A large gin and tonic with ice, and you can have one as well," she said, giggling again. I got the two drinks and we sat down. I sipped my drink and lay back in the chair. "You tired, darling?" she asked.

"I'm not too bad."

"That's good," she said with that suggestive smile again.

We had another drink, then went up to the room about an hour later. Margaret was soon undressed and in the shower, and minutes later, she called out, "Would you please come and wash my back?" And into the bathroom I went.

The next morning, it was about ten when the first exhibitor came in. Margaret went straight over to him, introduced herself, then showed him to his space. He seemed happy, so I carried on with finishing the graphics thinking that Margaret was far better in meeting the exhibitors than I was.

Gradually all the exhibitors came in, and my Margaret was doing a grand job. I finished putting up the graphics and went to join her. "You alright, my love?"

"Yes, Tel, no problems. They all seem happy and are nice."

"Meeting you does that," I said.

"There you go again, rose-coloured specks."

"Give us a kiss," I said, and Margaret obliged. We then wandered round and told them we would be in the bar to have a drink and sandwich if anyone wanted us, and off we went to the bar for about an hour or so.

When we went back, they all seemed very happy. They thanked us for a good job and said it was so nice to go on site and find everything ready for them. Margaret said, "I hope you will remember that next time your company needs a stand," and gave them one of our cards. *What a great PR lady she is.*

Another early breakfast then I went into the exhibition for a quick check round. All was well. Margaret was behind the reception sorting out the guest book and placing out the list of exhibitors. At the side of the hall opposite the bar, the tables were being set up for the buffet. Gradually the exhibitors trickled in. That was it; we just needed the visitors. It was just after eleven that the first visitor came in, but soon after more arrived and it gradually started to get busy.

Margaret was having a great time on reception, chatting and giggling to all the visitors. I went over and said, "You're enjoying yourself, love."

"Yes, it's quite fun, but it makes you thirsty."

"OK, what would you like?"

"A small lager please, darling. Then when you bring it over, come round the counter, and I will give the waiter a kiss."

"So that's what I am now, a waiter?" I said, laughing. I came back with two drinks, a pint for me and a half for Margaret, went round the counter, and said, "I'm waiting."

Margaret looked at me, giggled, and said, "You don't forget anything, do you?" I sat with her while we sipped at our drinks.

"Seems to be going well," I said.

"Yes, there has been quite a lot of visitors signed in. Let's hope the exhibitors are doing good business," Margaret answered, as she finished her drink.

"Would you like another?" I asked.

"Why, do you want another kiss?"

"I wouldn't say no."

"Go on, then. I will have another half."

"Did you want a sandwich?"

"Why, do you want two kisses?"

I laughed. "I will bring you over a sandwich with your lager, and when I took the drink and eats over, I got my reward.

The day soon went. We asked some of the exhibitors how they had done, and all seemed pretty happy. After all had left, I locked up and we went to the bar for a relaxing drink or two.

The following morning, we had early breakfast again. In the hall, I checked that all was OK. Margaret again went behind the reception, and at about ten, I took a cup of coffee over to her. Then I went up to get changed into my dinner suit, as my train to London was midday.

On arriving at Euston station, I got a taxi to my flat to check my mail and answer machine, then I rang my mate to let him know where I was. I went down to wait for him, and up he came in his white Lotus sports car. I got in and said, "You're still a flash bastard."

"Yeah, did you have a good run down?"

"Not bad." About fifteen minutes later, we arrived at the Liverpool street station hotel where the Masonic temple was. We were a little bit early, so we had a drink in the bar, and we weren't the only early birds.

The meeting went well, and the festive board was a nice meal. About ten, I had to leave, but outside, I just couldn't get a taxi. There were none about. I thought it strange outside a big railway station. I didn't really want to get on the tube in a dinner suit, but time was pushing on so I had to get on. I got to Euston with eight minutes to spare. I rang the hotel and said to the receptionist, "Please would you tell Mrs Parker I'm on my way and to leave the room keys at reception for me when she goes to bed?"

"OK," the receptionist said. I hung up and had to run for the train.

On getting back to the hotel in the early hours, I went to the reception for the room keys. The lady told me that my wife was in the residents' lounge. I thought, *Silly cow, she should have gone to bed.* I went in the lounge, and Margaret was talking to one of the exhibitors. She got up and ran over to me, threw her arms round me, kissed me very hard, and started crying.

"What the hell is going on, and why are you sitting in here with him?"

"Tel, please come and sit down. I have gotten you a large brandy."

"What's going on?" I shouted.

"Sit and drink the brandy, and I will tell you." The chap got up and said he would see us in the morning. I sat down and threw the brandy down in one go. Bloody hell, it burnt. "Right, what's going on?"

Margaret got hold of my hand. She still had tears in her eyes. "Tel, there has been an explosion at your flat, and you have got to ring the police in Hackney."

"What do you mean?"

"I went to the room after I had my dinner and didn't fancy anything on the telly, so I put on the radio and a newsflash came through that there had been an explosion at a minicab office in Hackney Road, London. Tel, I was so worried, as you said you might go back there." She started to cry heavy again.

"Come on, love, I'm here with you." I then picked up the phone and ordered two large brandies. "Right, love, what happened next?"

"I asked the reception to get me the Hackney Road police station. I told them that you may have been in there." She started to cry heavy again, and a waiter then came up with the brandies.

"Sip this," I said. "You'll feel better."

She did, then she went on to say that when she got the message that I was on my way, it was the greatest. She stopped, as she couldn't talk for crying. I cuddled her and wiped away her tears. She looked up at me and burst out crying again. "Tel, I thought I had lost you," she said, and she pulled me tight to her.

After about five minutes, Margaret was beginning to steady herself and told me that I had to ring the police as soon as I got in. I picked up the phone and asked the receptionist to get me Hackney Road police station. Minutes later, I was through to the police. They wanted to know where I was that evening, when I was last at the flat, and when would I be back in London. I gave them all the details they wanted and they asked me to go to the station on my return on Saturday. I said I would and hung up, and then I looked at my Margaret. She still had tearful eyes. I cuddled her, I gave her a kiss, and she started crying again. "What am I going to do with you, my love?" I said. "Come on, where's your saying 'don't worry be happy' gone?"

She tried to smile and said, "Tel, I love you so much."

"Come on, darling, let's go up and see if we can grab a bit of sleep."

We went up to the room, undressed, and got into bed. Margaret snuggled up to me and we tried to sleep, but we were both awake at six after a couple of bad hours. We took a shower and then wondered what to do next. I decided to ring my mate to ask him to go and collect my stuff at the flat. Margaret reminded me that we still had the exhibition to run, and then she gave me a weak smile.

After my shower I got dressed and rang my mate. "Hi, Tel. You're early, what's up?"

"My flat has been blown up."

"Fucking hell, sorry man," he said.

"Can you get over and pick up all my stuff?" I said.

"Yeah mate, I'm on my way. Give us your phone number, and I will give you a call when I've got it." I gave him the number and hung up.

On the way to breakfast, I told reception that I was expecting an urgent phone call. We went in the breakfast room, but we didn't eat much; both of our tums were bubbling, so I ordered two brandies. We poured them in our coffees and drank them, then we went to the banquet room.

About two hours later, I was paged. I went to the phone and the reception put me through to my mate. "Tel, babes," he said, "there ain't nothing there. It's just a great big space and a pile of rubble."

"There must be something."

"No, nothing. Everything is gone, as said, just rubble and bricks."

"OK mate, thanks. I will see you when we get back to London." I put the phone down and went over to Margaret and told her.

"God, what we going to do, Tel? You have lost everything; also, you switched the insurance."

"Yes I know, love, but we have most of our clients' phone numbers and addresses at home."

"But all your drawings, who owes you money, who you owe money to – Tel, it's a terrible mess."

"I know, love," I said.

By this time the word had gotten round the exhibition, and the exhibitors were coming over to us giving their support and offering any help or equipment we needed. I ordered more coffee and brandy, and just as the waiter brought them over, the first visitor came in. Margaret said good morning and got him to sign in. *Good*, I thought, *this will help her get over this terrible shock*. Then some more came in, so the exhibition was again under way. We sipped our brandy coffee, and Margaret said, "In one respect, we are lucky."

I looked at her and asked, "How do you work that out, my love?"

"First, Tel, you weren't at the flat, thank God. Second, this is an office and drawing-office exhibition, so we will take up the exhibitors' offers and see what we can get at good prices. I will make a list of what I will want and you do the same, then we will go round and talk to them."

We did, and they were very good and helpful. As you may have guessed, my list was the biggest, with all drawing instruments, brushes, paints, board, paper, and such, but the biggest thing was a large drawing board. The company that was exhibiting these had a beautiful one with parallel movement and floating adjustment. I had a chat with the gent in charge of the stand. He was very kind and let me have it as an exhibition-soiled second at 75 per cent off. "You and your wife have been so helpful to us all. Nothing is too much trouble."

The rest of the exhibitors were all the same, and we both felt a little better. Margaret asked me to look after the reception for a while, and she then went round to thank them all. She came back looking more her old self. When I said that she looked better, she smiled and said, "I got a lot of kisses." Then she giggled and said, "Tel, don't worry, be happy. Give us a kiss." I do what I'm asked.

The rest of the day was quiet. Then was it time to lock up for the day. Tomorrow would be the last day, finishing at four, then the pull out and load up. As one of the exhibitors who had electric typewriters on his stand was going out, I asked him what type of a deal I could get on a nice typewriter. He said, "I will have a think and let you know tomorrow, but because of your terrible problem it will be a good price."

I thanked him and went and told Margaret. "Ooh, Tel, that would be lovely if we can afford one. And if it's one of those with a golfball system, you will be able to use it for typesetting and save time and money on Letraset."

We went to the bar for well-needed gin and tonics. I took them over to where Margaret was sitting, but before I sat down I went across to the gent I had spoken to about the electric typewriter and said, "Margaret would like one with a golfball system."

He laughed. "I thought she might. We have a new model coming out in about six months, so the one on show – not the one being used as a demo, the one standing on its box – I will let you have it at half price."

I shook his hand and said, "Done. Now would you like a drink?"

"Thanks, Terry. A small scotch." I got him a large one. Margaret was over the moon when I told her, and she shouted her thanks over to him.

After another drink we went into dine, both feeling better than we did earlier. After a nice meal and a bottle of wine, I got two more drinks to take up to our room. In the room, Margaret said, "I'm glad you sorted it all out, Tel." Then she came over to me as she was undoing her blouse, pulled me tight, and kissed me hard. "Tel," she whispered, "you're not too tired are you?" I kissed her back and said no.

The following morning, only a few visitors came in and about three of the exhibitors started to pack up. Some said they would be contacting us regarding shows in the main exhibition halls round the country, so we gave them our card. Margaret went back to the reception to collect all the visitors' details she had to send onto the exhibitors when we got back, and I started to get all the equipment we bought into one area, with the exception of the drawing board, as I would have to dismantle it.

Once all the exhibitors had left, Margaret was on her hands and knees, picking up paperclips, elastic bands, pencils, ballpoint pens, and such that had been left. She also found a big pack of envelopes.

I said to her, "Say one for me."

"Shut up."

I just laughed and said, "While you're on your hands and knees, you have a lovely bum."

"If I have, you can leave it alone, as its mine."

"Really?" I answered.

"Well, maybe later I might consider a little bit of persuading." She giggled and carried on picking up paperclips.

About half an hour later, while we were having a rest with a cold lager, the driver and lads turned up. I got them all a beer then told them what had happened. They were quite shocked. I asked if they would be able to drop some stuff at my new studio in Blythe road on Saturday afternoon, and they agreed to help out.

After they had their beer, they started to take everything down, and while they did so, Margaret and I started unclipping the spotlights and dismantling the shell scheme. By nine thirty, everything was loaded, so I treated the lads to some grub at a small buffet-type restaurant that was open twenty-four hours.

When we had all eaten, Margaret and I wished them a safe journey and went up to the bar for a nightcap. "What a week," I said to Margaret. She looked at me with those big brown eyes and just said, "Don't."

I got another drink to take up with us and up to the room we went. I put the drinks on the bedside tables, then sat on the bed. "Are you alright?" Margaret asked.

"Yes, love," I answered. "I'm just thinking what a lot of sorting out we have to do next week."

"Come on, Tel. Get undressed and get in bed; I need a cuddle. We can talk on the way home tomorrow."

"OK, love," I said, quickly getting undressed. I had a sip of my drink.

"You can drink that later," Margaret said. I slipped into bed, and Margaret snuggled up to me.

I said, "You're lovely and warm, love."

"You're not," she said, giggling, "but I will soon get you warm." And she did.

On arriving back to London, we had time to put our bags at home and have a cup of coffee before we went to the studio just round the corner. Margaret was very impressed by what I had done, as it was the first time she had seen the studio since I'd done the flap and carpet and arranged the furniture.

"Tel, you have done a good job, as always."

"Thanks, love," I said, and I just looked at her.

"What's the matter, Tel?" Margaret asked.

"Nothing."

"Tel, you're telling me porkies; I know you too well."

I put out my hands and said, "Come here, darling." She came over, and I pulled her close to me, kissed her hard, and said, "I love you so much, Margaret. I just wouldn't be able to live without you. You have stood by me through this problem with loving support."

"Tel, you are my life. We have a great thing to be so much in love – millions would love to have it, but they haven't. Tel, I know ours will live forever." Margaret kissed me hard, and we were still cuddling when the driver came in.

"Sorry to interrupt you two lovebirds, but I have a delivery to make."

After the lads had finished and left, I told Margaret we had better get over to see the police in Hackney, so I locked up and off we went. At the police station, we saw the inspector in charge, and he told us that a body had been found in the rubble. It was the Maltese chap who had the flat under mine. The inspector said they would let us know when the inquest would be.

We then went on to see the flat. My mate had been right; there was nothing there, just a big gap. Margaret squeezed my hand. "Tel," she said, "It's awful."

"Yes, love, let's go from this place of horror and death." We headed home, and I pulled up at the off-licence for a couple of bottles of wine. After we unpacked, I went and picked up some fish and chips for dinner.

After dinner we sat and told Ralph all about what had happened. He told me that I had been very lucky – I could have been in there. "Yes," I said. Margaret squeezed my knee, and she had tears in her eyes. I put my arm round her. She put her head on my shoulder and just said, "Tel."

A couple of minutes later, Ralph left. I said to Margaret "Are you OK now, love?"

"Yes, Tel, but I just can't help thinking of what could have happened."

"Now listen, darling, it didn't and we are together." I kissed her then said, "On Monday, could you ring all our clients, contractors, suppliers, et cetera, on what has happened? I'll get my drawing board and area sorted out and run an electric supply to your desk for your new typewriter."

"Ooh, yes," she said. "I had forgotten about that."

"That's cheered you up, a new toy to play with."

"So have you, with your new drawing board."

We rested on Sunday, as we knew that Monday was going to be a busy day for both of us. The day went fast. Margaret worked very hard; she only stopped for a quick sandwich. She was on the phone nearly all day, got my drawing board in place, sorted out my working area, then started on doing the electrics. Come six we had finished what we wanted to but were well knackered.

"Let's go now and have a drink," I said.

"OK, love. That sounds fine. Let's go – I'm gasping," she said, blowing me a kiss.

"Is that all I get?"

"Come here, then," she replied. I went over and got my reward.

I got Margaret a half of lager, and I had a pint. Before I was halfway done, Margaret said, "Please, Tel, can I have another?"

"Yeah, you were gasping." I got another two halves and sat down. "There is a very important thing that we haven't discussed." Margaret looked puzzled. "Your wages."

"There is plenty of time to talk about that once we have everything sorted out, and as you know, darling, I'm very happy." Then she winked at me.

"You're a naughty girl," I said.

"You wouldn't want me any other way," she said and started to giggle.

"What's the matter with you – have you a feather in your knickers?"

"If I had, would you take it out?" she said, giggling again.

"I'm going to have trouble with you tonight, I can see," I said.

"You bet you are."

The next two weeks seemed to go well. After we sorted everything out, we were on track. Work was coming in, and some stands were confirmed and being built. I said to Margaret, "Fancy going to Malta for a week?"

She looked at me. "Are you serious?"

"Yes," I said, "it will do us a world of good. Also, we haven't got to be on site till about a month's time."

"Is the place free?"

"I don't know, I will give John a ring." Ten minutes later, I was off the phone. It was free.

"Tel, you're a bugger."

"I know. I will pop up to the travel agent to see what flight I can get. Would you ring your friend who used to work at the design council and see if she would like to run the studio while we are away?"

"OK, love, but you're still a bugger." I laughed and out I went. An hour later, Margaret's friend had agreed to look after the studio, and we had a flight at ten thirty a.m. in ten days' time with Air Malta.

The day before we were due to go, Margaret's friend came to the studio, and we showed her how to work the answer machine and the alarm system. I gave her a spare set of keys and the phone number of the flat in Malta, just in case of emergency, but I thought, *What the hell could I do in Malta if there was a problem?* I then went over to the greengrocer's to let him know what was happening, and he said he would keep an eye on the studio.

We arrived in Malta bubbling like a couple of teenagers. The same guy as before picked us up at the airport, and we dumped our gear in the apartment and went over to the bar opposite. They all greeted us as old friends; it was like coming home. As soon as we got in, I started to open the cold champagne, and Margaret came out of the bedroom in only her open light blouse and small briefs. "It's hot, darling," she said.

I looked at her and said, "Yes, I know. Shall we go up on the roof and toast Malta with champagne?"

"What a good idea," she answered and walked to the roof door. I took off my shirt, picked up two glasses and the half-opened bottle, and went up on the roof.

"Tel, it's so lovely and warm up here. This is just marvellous." I pulled the champagne cork, and Margaret said, "Goodnight, darling. No, not yet," and started to giggle. We toasted "to love" then sipped the drink. Margaret pulled me close, her bare breasts through her open blouse pushing against my chest. She just said, "Tel," and kissed me on the neck. I pulled her even tighter and kissed her long and lovingly. Margaret took my hand and we went back down to the bedroom.

The following morning, we woke about six. I got up and put on the kettle to make coffee, and then I noticed the champagne was still half full. Then I had a wicked idea and chuckled to myself. I must have made a noise, as Margaret woke up. "I have put the kettle on for coffee," I told her.

"Go boy," she said, "but you have a wicked look in your eye, so out with it."

"Well, darling, when we were last in the Grand, one of the waiters told me the best way to drink champagne with a lady is to have it room temperature."

Margaret said, "Go on."

"Well, you pour it over your naked lady and drink it off her."

"Oh really?" Margaret said. Then she pulled back the sheet. "What are you waiting for?"

So I got the warm champagne poured some over her and started to drink. Yes, I could understand what he'd said. After I was done, Margaret asked if there was any left. "Yes, about a third of a bottle," I replied.

"Good," she said. "Now it's my turn." What can I say? I had to oblige, like a good boy.

Two days later, we were just getting ready to go out when the phone went. I looked at Margaret and shrugged my shoulders. I picked it up and said hallo.

"Is that you, Terry?" It was the young girl who was looking after the studio. "Your bank wants you to ring them as soon as you can," she said, and she gave me the number. I thanked her and hung up.

I got through to the bank, told them who I was and where I was calling from, then asked to speak to the manager. (He knew me well, as he was the same manager I'd dealt with when I first started.)

"Hallo, Terry, what have you been up to?" he asked.

"Nothing, why?" I said.

"Well, Terry, your company has been frozen. You owe a firm £1000, and you haven't paid them."

"God, it's one we forgot because of the blow up! I will get in touch with someone to get it paid straight away."

"Good, but your company will still stay frozen until it's all sorted out."

"What does that mean?"

"You can't put any money in or take any out, but I will sort something out for you."

"We will get a flight home."

"No, finish your holiday, as there is nothing you can do if you rush home."

"OK. I will let you know if I can get it paid." I said goodbye, hung up, and then told Margaret.

"Tel, how much more bad luck are we going to have?"

"I don't know darling; I didn't think things could get worse – how wrong could I be?"

Margaret came over, put her arms round me, and said, "I'm here with you, Tel. We will get over this together. Remember, don't worry; be happy."

"I'll try," I said and kissed her. I picked up the phone and rang the studio. I asked the girl to look at our phone number book and gave her the name of my friend and client that we'd done the Manchester exhibition for. When I told him the problem, he asked how he could help. I told him the name of the company that we hadn't paid and asked him to contact them, find out the details, and pay them for me.

"No problem, Terry. Give me a ring in a couple of hours' time, and I will let you know how I get on."

I said, "Thank you so much," and hung up. Margaret asked how I got on. "OK," I said.

"You're lucky to have such a good friend in a client."

"I have known him for years and worked hard for him to build up his company, and yes, we are good friends."

"I will pour you a drink now; you must need it."

I nodded. We drank a bottle of wine in no time at all. Then Margaret said, "Let's go over to the shop and get something for lunch, as you have to make some phone calls later."

"OK, love," I replied. So over to the store we went, trying to look happy.

We got some bacon, their Hobser crusty bread, and some more wine. We only had a couple of bottles in the fridge, and we knew they wouldn't last long in the mood we were in.

We went up on the roof for lunch in the lovely sunshine. "I don't think it will be too bad, if the company we owe the money to lets my friend pay it," I said to Margaret. "Also, my bank manager is quite clever, and he will find a way round the problem I'm sure."

"I'm certain you're right, love," Margaret said. "Also, it can't be worse than what we have already been through."

"Yes, I suppose so, but it is such a bad start for you – giving up a good job and coming in with me, then all this happens. I feel so bad about it."

"Tel, it's not your fault, and look, we are together. This is what we both want in life, so we take the rough with the smooth, smile, and carry on. Come on, let's go down and find out if all is going well with the plan."

I first rang my friend to find out if the company would accept payment from him. "Enjoy the rest of your holiday, Terry. They have accepted me paying them, a cheque is on its way, and they will send me the paperwork on receipt of the cheque."

I thanked him and told him we would come and see him on our return. I then rang the bank and told the manager. He had worked out a way for us to still trade and said we should go and see him as soon as we can on our return.

After I hung up, I looked at my Margaret and said, "All OK and done." She came over, gave me a big kiss and cuddle, and said, "Let's have another glass then go down to the beach to cool off."

"Sounds good to me," I said. We drank our wine, and off we went to the little beach. We went there every day. The water was lovely. We just larked about, splashing and cuddling like a couple of kids without a worry in the world.

We arrived back in the UK in the late afternoon, got a taxi home, plonked in the cases, and went straight round to the studio. The young girl was pleased to see us and asked if we'd had a good time. We laughed. "I know, that was a silly thing to say," she said.

"Yes, it wasn't too bad, considering," Margaret said.

We looked at the post – a couple of bills and four nice big cheques. I rang my bank and spoke to the manager to let him know we were home and had some cheques to put in. "Bring them over tomorrow morning, and I will explain how we can put them in an account that you can use," he said.

I said we would be there by eleven, and then I rang my client friend to let him know we were back. I told him we were seeing the bank manager the next morning and, subject to what he said, would be able to send a cheque off to him for the amount he covered for me.

"No problem, Terry. Next week will do," he said.

"OK, but you know me – I like to pay my bills quickly." I thanked him and hung up. "Right, what else is there to do?" I said to Margaret.

"Pay the young lady for looking after the studio," she said.

"Sorry, I forgot," I said. "I will give you a personal cheque." I put another ten quid on it and gave it to her.

"That's ever so kind of you, Terry," she said.

Margaret chipped in and said, "He's lovely."

"Who's got rose-coloured specks now?" I said. We all laughed, then said our goodbyes, locked up, and went back home.

As soon as we got in, I went to the fridge, took a bottle of wine out, and poured two glasses. "Things seem to be sorting themselves out," I said.

"I hope so, darling. You're under so much pressure." She came over gave me a cuddle and kiss.

We were still embracing when in came Ralph. "Still at it, then," he said. We both said, "Shut up," and thumped him.

After dinner, Margaret put on the telly in the front room. I got some ice out of the fridge and made two very large gin and tonics. I gave one to Margaret and we said cheers.

"Bloody hell, darling, they're strong. What're you trying to do, get your wicked ways with me?" Margaret said, giggling. I just looked her straight in the eyes and said yes. "You don't beat about the bush, do you?" she replied.

"No."

Then she really started giggling. "Pack it up, you'll make me wet my knickers."

"Take them off, then."

"Ooh, you would love that."

"So would you," I replied.

"Tel, you get very cheeky when you're in this type of mood, so I think I will have to cool you down with a kiss."

"If you think that will cool me down, you're welcome to try."

"You're a bugger. That's all you're waiting for."

"Fifth amendment," I said. She slid over to me and kissed me passionately.

"Tel, my darling, we will make it, I promise."

I kissed her back just as passionately. "When my divorce comes through, I'm going to marry you."

She kissed me again and said, "You have to ask me first, as I might find a better offer." She started giggling again.

"Please yourself," I said as I finished my drink. "Would you like another g and t?"

"Just a small one to take to bed with me, as I want to give you your answer, if and when you ask me to marry you."

"OK, I will bring it up."

By the time I got up, Margaret was in bed in her Calvin Kline attar. I snuggled up to her, and she kissed me and said, "Tel, love me."

I awoke suddenly to a bang; it was the street door, Ralph going to work. I looked across at my Margaret. She was sleeping soundly, so I slipped out of bed and went downstairs to make some coffee. When it was ready, I poured myself a cup and while sipping it, I started to think of what we had to do. First, we had to go to the bank. Second, I had to ring up my stand contractor to see if all was on track with the stand I had at the NEC. Third, I had to ring up my client who had paid the company we owed money to. Last, I had to sort out what other work we had to do.

At the bank, the manager saw us straight away. He had set up another account so that any cheques I got could be paid into the new account. He told me I would have to speak to my solicitor to get the company cleared, and it would possibly be a court case. Margaret and I looked at one another. "Sorry," he said, "but that's how the law works. But it's been paid now, so you should have no trouble." We all shook hands and left.

Walking back to the car, I said to Margaret, "I didn't expect that."

"Nor did I," she answered.

Back at the studio, I rang my contractor, and all was well. The carpet was down, and they were well under way. My next call was to my solicitor. I gave him all the details, and he said that he would find out all about it and give me a ring. I looked at Margaret, who was typing away, and said, "Darling, I'm shattered. Let's stop for an hour and go to the pub for a beer and sandwich."

"What a good idea."

I got two lagers and a couple rounds of sandwiches. We found a quiet corner and sat. I took a big swig of my drink then said, "So far, so good."

"Yes," Margaret answered, "and all's well at the NEC?"

"Yeah, let's hope it stays that way. We have had enough bad news to last a lifetime."

"You can say that again," she said. We finished the food had one more drink and went back to the studio. I rang the client who'd paid the money for me and told him that I would send a cheque in five days, when the cheques I had put in the new company had cleared. He said that would be no problem.

I looked across at Margaret. "Fancy a cup of coffee, love?"

"Yes please, Tel. You know, we will have to get a coffee maker so we can have good coffee all day."

"That's a good idea. We will leave a little early and go up to the shops at the Bush and get one," I answered.

"We can go in the supermarket and get some supplies also; we will need some ground coffee."

I chipped in and said, "Also some wine!" We both laughed.

The next few days went well. I finished a design and took it to the client. He liked it and it was in his budget, so we got it. Friday morning we were off to the NEC about mid morning. The contractor rang and said there was a rumour going round the halls that I was in trouble, money-wise. I explained to him, and after I hung up, Margaret asked, "What was that all about?"

I told her, and she said, "Bloody rumours."

"Don't worry, love, leave it to me. There is a way round it." I picked up the phone and rang my mate Chas, who had the van-hire firm. I told him what had happened and asked if he could cash a cheque for a thousand pounds if I brought one round about ten that morning.

"No problem, Tel. I'll have it here by then."

"Great. See ya then."

Margaret was one jump in front of me. "I know what you're up to; we will go in the bar at the NEC, you'll flash the cash for all to see, and all who know you will see all is OK."

"Got it in one, darling. Right, let's get going." I locked the studio and off we went.

We got to the NEC at twelve thirty. We went to the bar, ordered a couple of drinks, took out the wad of notes, and peeled off a ten. A couple of minutes later, in came my carpet layer with his daughter and her boyfriend. We all said our hallos, and I took out the bundle again, peeled off another ten, gave it to him and said, "Get yourself a drink and sit down." While we were in the bar, a couple of contractors came in, so I went over and bought them drinks, getting the bundle out every time. I looked at Margaret, and she smiled. "All OK, love?" she said.

"Yes, my pet. It is now," I answered.

She smiled again and said, "Good."

We went back to the stand. The phone had now been connected. Margaret said she would ring the client to give him the number and to tell him the stand was finished and ready for him. "OK, love," I said, and I gave her a quick peck on the cheek.

She giggled and said, "A couple of drinks make you randy."

"Shut up." I laughed.

The lads came over and asked me if I would have a look round to see if there was anything else to be done. Everything looked good, so we went back to the lads, gave them a good drink, and asked if there would be anyone about tomorrow. They said there would be a couple of lads on their other stand, fixing up the clients' equipment. We said goodbye and they left. We then pushed off and decided to call in the Malt Shovel, where all the exhibition lads drank, on the way to the hotel. As we walked in, my carpet contractor called us over. "What're you having?"

"Two g and t," I said.

"Sit down with us. I will bring them over." We sat with the two lovebirds, his daughter and her chap – mind you, we can't shout; we cuddled and kissed all the time. The contractor returned with two very large g and t, and we all said cheers. "Well, how's things going with you two now? Have you gotten over the blow up?"

"Well, so-so," I answered.

"As your dear friends. we can tell you, after we heard, we just couldn't believe such bad luck. "Let's hope that's the last of it and things start to get better for you both."

"It will," Margaret said, "as we have one another, and nothing will ever part us."

They agreed. "We know you're inseparable. It's lovely to see such love and devotion."

Several months passed. We were becoming well known for good design and service, and quite a lot of work was coming in. My divorce came through, and I exchanged the Jag for a brand-new white Scimitar GTE company car. Then Ralph moved to York, where his brother lived. Things going well and we were very happy.

Then bad luck struck again. We got up one morning to find the car had been vandalised. Black paint had been thrown all over it. It was reported to the police, and they took a sample of the paint. It was the same type of paint they used in tyre-fitting firms. I had a good idea of who'd done it, but I couldn't prove it.

Then, a few weeks later, while we were at the studio just round the corner, we were burgled. We got home and the place was a mess. We called the police, but there was not much they could do. The only thing that was stolen was Margaret's jewellery, an old tape recorder, and a case, but my Margaret took it very badly. The following day, she cried nearly all morning and threw all her underclothes away. I comforted her and took her out in the afternoon to buy new clothes – more pressure that we didn't need, but we had been there before. We had one another, so it didn't get us down.

Then we expanded. Ken, a sign writer and expanding poly lettering cutter who'd done all our exhibition graphic work, told us that the shed where he worked was getting too small, so we suggested that he could have our back room free of charge and a part doing all our work; he would give us a price for all his work, and we would pay him. Then it would go through us with a percentage that Margaret would run, and we would invoice the client.

He agreed, as we would then be the only company he would have to invoice, which would make his life easier. We all shook hands, and Margaret and I struck and registered the new company, named "Margraph". Also, all the graphic work I did would go through Margraph. It worked well also if we were out meeting a client, for example, Ken could answer the phone. He loved a drink and thought the world of my Margaret (mind you, so did everyone else). He became a very dear friend, and we had some wonderful times on site.

Now for a shock for my Margaret. We were at the NEC and had two stands nearly finished. Ken had some more graphics to put up, but everything was going well, so at lunchtime we all met in the press bar for drinks – my carpet contractor, his daughter, her chap, and Ken. We were all having a good laugh. I was at the bar getting a drink, and Margaret was chatting to the contractor's daughter. The boyfriend said they were getting married and asked me be his best man.

"What a lovely thing to ask me. I would be honoured," I said, and I shook his hand.

He then looked at me and said, "When are you going to get hitched?"

"I haven't proposed yet," I answered.

"Well, go and do it now," he said, looking me straight in the eyes. "Or have you no bottle?"

"OK," I said. "Be back in a minute to pay for the drinks." I went over to Margaret and said to her, "Please love, would you stand up a second?"

She looked at me, puzzled, and stood up. I went down on one knee and took hold of her hand; it all went very quiet. "Margaret, my lovely darling, please will you marry me?"

"Yes, my Tel. Yes, I will."

"But there is one condition – that we marry on my birthday so I will never forget the wonderful day we married."

She gave me a gentle slap round the head and lifted me up. "I'm so happy. I have dreamed for this day to come!"

"So have I." We kissed again, and as we broke away, we could hear the champagne corks popping. Margaret whispered in my ear, "Good night, darling… later."

Then everyone came over to congratulate us, saying it was about time. I looked at Margaret and said, "Where will we have the reception?"

She looked at me and said, "Tel, I don't have to tell you, as you know."

I nodded and said, "And our wedding reception will be…" I paused. Margaret squeezed my hand. "At the Grand Hotel in Brighton, and you're all invited." Margaret kissed me again.

We went back to the hall. On arriving at the stand, we were met by the big boss. "Margaret and Terry," he said, "I would like to thank you for a great job. The stand looks good and you finished well on time. When you send your invoice, address it to me and you will be paid by return."

Before I could answer, Margaret replied, "Thank you, and it's a great day for me, as my wonderful Tel has proposed to me!"

"That's a must, as you're such a lovely, well-matched couple. Please, come into our bar and have a drink – you know where it is." We went in and had a drink and a chat with him. As he left, he said, "Don't forget; send the invoice to me. Also, I want to book you to design our next stand." We shook hands and he kissed Margaret on the cheek, looked across at me, and said, "Terry, you look after this wonderful lady."

"Don't worry, I will," I answered, then I took hold of Margaret hand and walked off.

We went to the other stand. It was all finished, and the client was putting his own bits of display up. Margaret told him we had just come back to check that everything was OK.

"Yes, Margaret. We are just fixing up a couple of our little displays and we will be finished. I would like to thank you both on doing a good job for us; it's the first time we had our stand completely finished well in front of time."

"We try hard," Margaret said. I walked over, shook his hand, and said, "We hope we can be of service to your company again."

"You can count on that," he said.

Getting in the car, Margaret said, "Tel, can we go straight back to the hotel and not stop at the Malt? I want you all to myself tonight."

I leant across and kissed her, then said, "Yes, I also just want to be with you, on our own."

She smiled. "Good."

When we got to the hotel, I said, "You check in, and I will go and order a couple of drinks at the bar." I got the drinks, put them on a little table, and as Margaret came over with the key and sat down, I said I would be back in a minute, as I wanted to take the cases up to the room.

"OK, love. I will see you in a mo," she answered. On the way to the room, I went to reception and asked them if they would send a bottle of champagne up to our room. She said it would be no problem, and it would be there in five minutes.

Back in the bar after taking the cases up, I said to Margaret, "It's been a wild day."

"No, Tel, it's been a lovely day. I just can't tell you how happy I am."

"Darling, I have wanted to ask you to marry me since you first told me to push off in that little restaurant." Margaret giggled. "Also, there's something else I have got to tell you." Margaret frowned. "There is another wedding – our carpet man's daughter, Annette, and Stuart. I have been asked to be best man."

"Tel, that's wonderful. He could be your best man."

"What a great idea," I answered. We finished our drinks, and I said, "Let's go and clean up to get ready for dinner."

"OK, love," she said, and up we went.

I opened the door to the room, leant in, and switched on the light. I stepped back to let Margaret go in first. As she walked in, she spotted the champagne. She turned round to me and said, "Tel, you're a bugger." She kissed me. "You think of everything.

"I try," I said, and I got another kiss. Then Margaret kicked off her shoes, flopped on the bed, and said, "Aren't you going to open it?"

I started to laugh. "I'm not going to go to sleep yet."

"Tel, we can get another bottle for later." She really started to giggle. I opened the bottle and we toasted each other and sipped the champs. I then said, "On Monday, we will go up to the bush and get you an engagement ring."

"Tel, I don't need a ring; I have you."

"Nonsense, I'm going to get you a ring."

"OK," she whispered, "can I have a kiss?" I kissed her then said, "Let's get ready and go down."

"OK. The sooner we eat, the sooner we can come up to bed, as I'm tired." She started to giggle again. We quickly got ready, finished up the pop, and went down. As I passed the reception, I ordered another bottle of fizz to the room. We had a nice dinner and chatted away about the stands and how pleased the clients had been. I also said we would have to book the register office for the wedding and go down the Grand to book a room for the reception, plus rooms for guests. We could do it on a bargain-break weekend.

Margaret giggled and said, "Oh God, the Grand again."

After dinner, we went straight up to our room, where the ice-cold bottle was waiting for us. Margaret switched on the telly while I opened the champers. There was another loud pop, and we looked at one another and started to giggle like a couple of silly kids.

As I was pouring the champers out, Margaret came over and put her arms round me, kissed me on the neck, and said, "Today, Tel, makes up for all the horrible things that happened to us in the past." I put down the bottle, pulled her close, and kissed her hard. Margaret then said, "I just don't want this day to go; it's the happiest in my life." She put her glass down and started to undo her blouse. "I need a cuddle, Tel, so let's go to bed."

"My lovely Margaret, I will give you cuddles forever; you're such a gorgeous, lovely lady to cuddle up to."

She pulled me to her and said, "You still wear rose-coloured specks, but I don't care."

"I love—" I started, but I couldn't finish, as she kissed me hard again.

The following morning we woke later than normal for us. I looked at the bottle on the side table; it was half-full. "Darling, coffee or champers?"

"Do you have to ask?"

"OK, I will make the coffee." She whacked me with a pillow, giggled, and said, "Don't push your luck just because you're engaged." I poured out the champers; it was still full of bubbles. I thought to myself, *Yes, I'm engaged to marry my wonderful lady.*

"What're you thinking, Tel?" Margaret asked.

"I'm just so happy, my love."

"Tel, last night was a lovely dream that I will keep in my heart forever." She put down her glass, ran round the bed, and cuddled and kissed me. As we parted I said, "You had better put some clothes on, or you will get cold."

She giggled and said, "You can talk."

"OK, you win," I answered.

We quickly showered, got dressed, and went down to breakfast. The waiter showed us to a table with a big bunch of flowers on it. We looked at one another, very puzzled, and sat down. Margaret took out the card. "Tel," she said, "it's from the carpet mob, congratulating us on our engagement. How sweet of them – they are such good friends."

"Yes," I said, "they are."

After breakfast, we soon packed and went down to check out. The receptionist said she would like to congratulate us on our engagement, on behalf of the hotel. We both thanked them and paid the bill. As we walked to the car, I said to Margaret, "That was nice of her."

"Yes," she said, and she started to laugh.

"What's so funny?" I asked.

"Well, Tel, we have been staying there for the last year as Mr and Mrs Parker."

"I didn't think of that," I said, then I started to really laugh.

"What's the matter now with you?" Margaret asked.

"Well, my love, wait till we go to the Grand to book a room for the reception."

She then burst out laughing again. "God, Tel, I didn't think of that. It's going to be really good fun when they find out."

When we got home, I leant over to her, kissed her very gently, and poured us a nice cold glass of wine. We had a couple of glasses then Margaret said she was going up to change. "OK," I said, "into Calvin Klein?"

"You're a cheeky bugger, Tel," she said. "You'd have a shock if I did come down like that."

"Would I?" She giggled and went upstairs.

As I was pouring another drink, Margaret walked in, smelling lovely. All she had on was one of my shirts, buttons opened just below the line of her breasts. She looked at me, did a sexy little giggle, and said, "I hope you don't mind me wearing one of your shirts, but I haven't got any nighties."

I took another swig of my wine. She giggled and said, "You must have something to eat after that long drive." She sat down and I went over and kissed the top of her breast. I said, "Yes, darling, I really need to bite onto something."

My shirt hung on her like a goddess. She pulled me to her and whispered, "Tel, we have something that is marvellous and wonderful that millions would love to have. We have got real love for each other, and the only way we can show it is by crying with happiness and being together all the time, now and forever, never ever to part, till our maker decides he needs us to help him in his job."

"Margaret, I just want to be with you forever."

"My darling Tel, I'm just the same. What we have is just paradise; let's keep it forever." I kissed her very softly. My shirt fell from her soft body, and Margaret looked up at me with half-closed eyes and said, "Tel, I love you with all my heart. Tel, love me."

Later I went into the kitchen thinking what a lucky bloke I was. At last, we were being favoured with a bit of happiness. I put the chops on the grill and heard a little voice shouting out, "Tel, would you like a drink?"

"Please," I replied.

"Good, get me one as well. It's in the fridge."

Caught again, I thought, so I got a bottle of wine out of the fridge and took it in. Margaret had put back on my shirt, but it wasn't buttoned up. I poured her a drink and said, "You should button up my shirt; you might get chilly."

"Please, darling, would you do it for me? It buttons up on a different side than a lady's."

"OK." I went over and started to button it up, carefully slipping my hand under her breast. She looked up at me and said, "Tel."

"What, darling?" I answered.

"I think you have missed a button lower down." She giggled.

"Margaret, I will sort that button out after we have had our evening meal, which if I don't go and sort out, will get overcooked."

"OK, we will eat first and you can fix my button later," she said, and she gave me a very seductive smile.

"My darling, I will be happy to fix your button later if you wish me so to do," I answered.

"How elegant you put it, dear sir. After my meal, I will await your service."

"Madame, I will do the washing-up first to make sure my hands are soft, my lady."

She tried to answer but couldn't stop laughing.

I went round to the studio at eight. I put on the coffee, and in walked Ken. "Alright, mate?" I asked.

"Yeah, how are you after the weekend?"

"Still on cloud nine," I said, laughing.

"I haven't known you two that long, but you are so well suited – you're just as one."

"Yes, Ken, everyone tells us this. We are a very lucky couple to be so much in love."

About an hour later, Margaret came in and Ken went over and congregated her. I had a small stand to finish off on the drawing board, but I could do that later, so I said to Margaret, "Come on, darling. Let's go to the registry office."

"OK, love."

"Won't be long," I said to Ken, and off we went.

We got a place on Friday at 10 a.m. on 7 May, 1982. When we came out of the office, Margaret kissed me and said, "Tel, you got your wish." I kissed her back and said, "Yes, darling, a day I will never forget."

She smiled. "It will be a happy day that I will never forget also."

"Right, love, let's now go and get a ring."

"Tel, you don't have to."

I just looked at her and said, "Margaret."

"Alright, love," she said and kissed me on the cheek.

Margaret picked out a lovely ring with three stones and engraving round the sides and a matching wedding ring. I paid the lady and we left, Margaret wearing her engagement ring.

On getting back to the studio, we checked on what was urgent, and Margaret rang the Grand to book a bargain weekend. She also booked a large suite for May the seventh and then asked if they would pencil in twenty double rooms on a bargain weekend for the same date. We would discuss the details at the weekend. "Tel, all booked for the wedding," she said.

I looked up from my drawing board. "Well done, love."

Friday soon came round. We worked till three, said bye to Ken, and off we went to Brighton. On arriving, we got our normal greeting, checked in, and we went to the bar while the porter took our bags up to our room.

Margaret said, "It's going to be great fun when they find out we are not married."

"They must get it all the time," I answered. Halfway through our drinks, in came the manager. "Hallo, Mr and Mrs Parker. Nice to see you again."

"It's nice to be back again," we said. "Could we tell you something in confidence?"

He nodded, so we told him. He smiled and said, "No problem, but they will all know on Saturday morning when we speak to the banqueting manageress." We both laughed, but we said we wanted to keep it quiet till then. "OK, I will make an appointment for you to see her at eleven tomorrow morning."

The following morning we got up later than the norm. We went down to breakfast and a lovely older lady who we knew quite well was our waitress. "Hello again," she said, "the usual?"

"Yes please," we said, and we asked her how she had been keeping.

"Not too bad," she answered and off she went. Within minutes, she was back with coffee and orange juice. A little later, up came Margaret's bacon and scrambled egg and the first of my very large kipper, toast, and crusty rolls. As I finished my kipper up came the second one. Margaret looked at me and said, "They really spoil you, Tel."

"You don't do too bad," I said, and we both laughed.

After breakfast, we went in the lounge and waited for the banqueting manageress. Half an hour later, this charming senior lady came over and said, "You must be Mr and Mrs Parker. You would like to look at one of our suites for a wedding reception?"

I didn't know what to say, but my Margaret just said, "Yes, please," and smiled at us both. We followed the lady to a beautiful suite. It was just the right size, perfect, a great big room with double doors leading to the en-suite bedroom. We both said, "That's fine; we would like to book it."

The lady smiled and asked, "Who is getting married?"

Now for the crunch, I thought. Margaret looked at the lady with one of her beautiful smiles and said, "Why, us of course."

The poor lady – I felt so sorry for her; she seemed so embarrassed.

"Oh, I see. If we go back down to the lounge, I will book it in," she said, so down we went and sat in the lounge with her. "Would you like a coffee or a drink?" she asked. The lady ordered a couple of pils lagers for us, and while we were filling in the order, the manager came over and asked if everything was OK, smiled, and winked. We said it was and the lady was looking after us well. When all the paperwork was done for the room, the lady said she would get the buffet details so we could pick what we would like, and off she went.

I looked at Margaret and said, "Poor lady." She just giggled. I said, "I can't get any sense out of you." She giggled again and said, "I'm just happy."

The lady then came back with the details. We worked out what we thought was a well-balanced buffet and some nice bubbly. She thanked us and said she would like to wish us all the best in the future and so would all the staff. "Also," she explained, "the manager has told me to let you know that, as you're very regular visitors, you will get a 10 per cent discount."

We thanked her for all her help, and she smiled then left. I looked at Margaret and said, "Didn't we do well?" Margaret just giggled. I thought, *I'm not going to get any sense out of her this weekend.* We finished our drinks and went out for a walk along the front, holding hands and chatting about how well things were going. We ended up at the famous Brighton Lanes and had a good look round, but we didn't buy anything.

We got back to the grand about five thirty, went to the bar for a quickie, then up to get ready for the evening dinner dance. When we walked into to the room, what a shock, there was a great big bouquet of flowers, a bottle of champagne in an ice bucket, and a box of chocolates with compliments of the Grand for our engagement. Margaret just burst into tears.

We showered and dressed, and decided to leave the champers till later. On the way to the bar, we stopped at the reception, and Margaret gave the lady a note she had written thanking all the staff. The lady thanked us and said it was a big surprise to them all. I said it was a big surprise to me too and laughed, ducking a swinging slap from my Margaret. I got hold of Margaret's hand and said, "Give us a kiss then." She obliged, and the lady said, "It's so lovely to see two people so happy."

We went into the bar and were again greeted with congratulations. I ordered two large dry martinis, and the bar steward served them up and said, "With the manager's complements." We thanked him and sat down at a little table. As we sipped our drink, I said to Margaret, "This is getting embarrassing."

"Darling, enjoy it – I am," she said, and she got hold of my hand. "Please, sir, can I have a kiss?" This time I obliged. On finishing our drinks, we went into the restaurant, and it was the same thing again. Then we were shown to a table right near the little three-piece band; they know us quite well, as we always danced a lot. They waved at us, and I waved back and Margaret blew a kiss.

As usual, we had a good meal, and while we were drinking our coffee, the leader of the little band said, "Tonight's is a special evening for two of our regular guests, as they have just got engaged to be married. And of course, the reception will be at their favourite hotel, here at the Grand. So would Terry and Margaret please start the dancing?" We got up to a lot of clapping, not just from the guests, but also the waiters. We danced well, and then others started to join us on the floor.

The evening went on till just past midnight. When it was all finished, we went over to the band and thanked them for a wonderful evening. The leader thanked us for our dancing and said, "Your jive routine is really good; you both work together perfect. But that's you two, you just are one."

Going up in the lift, I said to my Margaret, "What a great night."

"Yes, darling, but it hasn't finished yet," she said and started to giggle.

We got in the room, and I said, "I will open the bottle."

"Please would you undo the back of my dress first?" Margaret asked. I unzipped her dress, she moved her shoulders, and the dress dropped to the floor. "And my bra, please, love." I unhooked it, and that fell to the floor. Margaret then turned, kissed me, and said, "Love me, Tel."

The following morning, we awoke again late. Margaret showered while I made some coffee; the bottle still hadn't been opened. *No problem*, I thought, *we will take it home with us.* Margaret came out of the shower with a towel round and said, "It's your turn now and thanks for the coffee."

"OK," I said, and as I passed her, I pulled off her towel and gave her a little tap on her bootie.

"More," she said and giggled.

"Later," I answered and went into the shower.

Sunday morning is a good day to drive, as the roads are quiet. We got back in time to have a couple in the local before time, then we went home, both thinking what a great weekend it had been.

The next morning, we were in the studio bright and early, about ten thirty. As Margaret was making the second lot of coffee, the phone rang – it was my carpet chap. "I wonder if you and Margaret would meet me at the little jazz club we sometimes go to; we can have a meal there and I can tell you about the arrangements for my daughter's wedding. I'm thinking of getting the jazz band to come up for a cabaret. Also, I wonder if you and your lovely lady would do a demonstration jive as part of the evening?"

"OK, me old mate, we will meet you there at eight, and I will have a chat with Margaret to sort something out. See ya then." I put down the phone told Margaret what was said.

"OK, love. Let me think about it, and I will work out a routine for us to dance to."

"Margaret, I said a bloody demo."

"Tel, trust me, you can do it. You have a white suit, tie, and shoes, also a black shirt. I have my twenties outfit. We will look good, and we can go to the dance club a couple of afternoons and do a couple of practise runs. Darling, be positive. Just remember – don't worry; be happy."

"OK love, I will be guided by you. You think I can do it, then I will."

"Tel, love, I don't think; I know."

We got to the jazz club just before eight. My carpet man was at the bar. "Two pils lagers?" he said. We nodded, sat down, and looked at the menu.

After the meal, our friend told us what was planned. All the close exhibition friends were booked in the hotel where the reception was being held, and cars were laid on to take them to the church and back. When guests first arrived at the hotel, if they wanted a drink or sandwich, they would go to the best man's room, where we would have sandwiches and ten cases of champers. "Thanks a lot," I said.

He laughed. "Well, you are our best friends. Now also, I have spoken to the band. They are OK for that weekend, so it's now for you two to sort how you want it played."

"Tel," Margaret said, "order another bottle of wine; I need it."

Our mate was still laughing and said, "I knew I could rely on you two lovebirds."

"Right," said Margaret, "now we take over."

"OK." He nodded.

"You will have to co-ordinate with the band, so when they arrive at the hotel, you get them up to their rooms. Then Tel will say it's OK for the married couple to go up and change, but not to come down till he tells them. Once they have gone, the band will come down and set up. While they are doing that, me and Tel will go up and change." She stopped and had a quick drink, then went on. "When we come back down, I will go on the stage – by the way is there a stage?" He nodded. "As I said," she continued, "I will go on the stage with the curtains drawn behind me, then Tel will ring through tell them to come down. As they enter, I will do a bit of a speech on the Leonard Sachs–style Old Time Music Hall. As I finish, the curtains will draw. The jazz band will start, Tel will run over lift me off the stage, and we will then do a demo jive. Then when that tune finishes, the band will start another. Me and Tel will then break away and go to the guests to get them up to dance. Well, what do you think?"

"I knew I could rely on you, Margaret. Let's have another bottle of wine, then you two can get up and show me what you're made of on that dance floor. I have to know if you're worth booking."

We both looked at him, and my Margaret said, "You know, you're a saucy sod." He just laughed.

Friday we were in the studio early. Margaret had a couple of letters and quotes to get done before she went on site, and I had to leave early for the law courts, which I was not looking forward to, although my brief said I had nothing to worry about. I had a quick cup of coffee, kissed my Margaret, and said I would see her on site later. As I was going through the door, Margaret shouted, "Tel, don't worry; be happy." I gave her half a smile and left for the court.

I arrived well early, went in, and sat with the brief. Nearly two hours later, we were called in. My brief told me to say nothing unless the judge asked something. We went in, and I was shaking. I was told to sit down, and the charge was read out. When it was finished, my brief stood up and said to the judge, "Mr Parker has never been served a summons, Your Honour."

The judge looked at the prosecuting brief and asked, "Is this true, and if so, why?"

The brief quickly looked at his notes and said, "Yes, as there was no place to serve it, as the building for it to be served had been blown up."

The judge looked at me, but before he could say anything, my brief jumped up again and said, "Also, Your Worship, once my client found out he owed this money, it was paid in full." He sat down.

The judge had a deep sigh. He looked at the prosecuting brief again and said, "Is this true?" The answer was again yes. The judge then said, in a very loud voice, "You are wasting my time. Case dismissed." He wacked down his gavel.

I thanked my brief, and he said, "I told you you had nothing to worry about." We shook hands, and I left, off to give Margaret the news in Olympia.

I quickly found the stand, went over to my Margaret, kissed her on the cheek, and asked if all was well. "Yes, darling, the client is well happy. We should be finished in about an hour. Now how did you get on, love?"

"Case dismissed," I said.

"Tel, darling, that's wonderful news." She threw her arms round my neck and gave me a big kiss. "I told you, don't worry; be happy," she said, and she kissed me again. Terry Parker Designs was back in business again.

I came out of the little stand office, and the MD said, "Everything is now finished, but before we lock it all up, we all are going to have a drink and would be honoured if you and your lovely lady would join us."

"We would love to," I said, and we sat for about an hour, drinking and chatting to the MD. He was interested in how we met and said that in all the couples that he had met, he had never seen a couple so devoted as us. He laughed and said, "It's hard for a man to say but I will – you're so much in love with each other."

I said, "Don't worry, I don't care who knows. I love my Margaret," and Margaret said, "I love my Tel."

He just said, "It's so lovely to see." We finished our drinks and we left very happy with the world.

The following couple of weeks, we were very busy. We had to work two weekends on the trot then it eased off a bit. So we decided to take a four-day weekend break in a hotel at Woolacombe that Margaret heard about at her dance club. It had a large ballroom with dancing every evening, and this would be good for us to get some practise in doing the jive. The hotel was quite nice; we had a nice room and the food was good, but in the dance hall, there were very few men. It was nearly all older ladies, and when they found out I could dance, I got no rest. In fact, one lady gave me her room number. Margaret kept giggling and said, "You wanted to practise."

"Yes, but with you."

"Don't worry; be happy. I will ask the band to play a couple of jives tomorrow evening."

After breakfast the following morning, we asked if we could go in the ballroom for an hour, as we wanted to practise some new steps. We worked for about an hour and half, and then Margaret said, "That's enough for now. We will try to go through it tonight if there is room. If not, we will just do a jive, but we will come in again tomorrow."

We sat to rest and chatted on what we were going to do with the rest of the day. It was nice and sunny outside, so I suggested a run down to Croyde Bay. It was a bay I used to go many years ago.

"OK, love, you know the area." So off we went. It hadn't changed much, except there were a lot more people there. We took off our shoes and held hands as we walked down to the beach. The sea was as still as wild as ever, with great big waves. We sat on the dunes, and Margaret said, "It's so beautiful. I can see why you loved it here." We sat for about an hour and then went for a paddle. Of course a big wave came in, and we got wet well above the knees.

On the way back to the car, there was a big family bar, so I suggested a quickie before we went on our way. Margaret squeezed my hand and nodded, so up the steps we went into the bar. It was a very big place, with lots of families in there for lunch. Margaret found a table, and I got two lagers. We sat chatting about where we would go next, then, quite loudly, the F-word was said at the next table to us.

There were seven or eight RAF lads sitting and drinking, and again it was said. Margaret called across, "Please, lads, could you mind your language, as there are families in the room?"

There was no answer. About five minutes later, one of the lads said *sod*. "Don't say that; the lady don't like it," one of the lads said, and they all laughed. This type of thing went on for about another five minutes; they were being very sarcastic. Then the F-word was said quite loud. Margaret stood up, and the room went silent. I turned my rings round and looked to work out if and where the trouble would come from. Then my Margaret said in a very loud voice, "Young man... if you do it as much as you say it, you would be dead by now." She sat down, and all the families clapped and cheered. The RAF lads all got up and walked out, and everybody cheered again. A bloke came over and insisted on buying us a drink; another lady said to me as she was leaving with her husband and kids, "Mister, you have some wonderful lady there; you look after her."

The next few days, we practised our routine in the morning, as it was impossible at the evening dances with all the old girls. My Margaret still found it highly amusing that I just couldn't get any rest. During the day we toured round and really enjoyed ourselves.

Back home at the studio, lots of messages had been left with Ken, most of them old clients wanting stand designs. There were also a couple of new ones, so within an hour the little holiday was forgotten and we where steaming again. I was finishing off work drawings for a stand, and Margaret was on the phone making appointments. I looked across at her and said, "It looks like we will be working the weekend." Margaret laughed went and got a cup of coffee, brought one over to me, and said, "Tell me something new. But love, we have some good clients. We can't moan." I nodded as I drank my coffee.

The next weeks flew by, and before we knew it, the Birmingham wedding was on us and we were punching up the motorway to the hotel. We checked in about four on the Friday afternoon and went to our small suite. On entering, we looked at each other – there were twelve cases of champers stacked in the corner. I went straight over to one, opened it, and put twelve bottles in the fridge. My Margaret said,

"Good thinking, Batman," and giggled. I kissed her and said, "Well, we want it chilled."

"Do we?" she answered still giggling.

"You behave yourself; we are not in Malta," I laughingly said.

She just looked at me, said, "Tel," and started to giggle again. "OK, but just this once I will be a good girl." We had a quick shower and changed. As Margaret was putting on her makeup, I opened a bottle of champers and poured out two glasses passing one to her. "Thanks, darling. I have a feeling this wedding is going to be a boozy-do," Margaret said as she took the glass.

"What do you expect, when all the exhibition mob get together," I answered.

"I don't know what you mean, Tel," she said and held out her empty glass, giggling again.

After polishing off the bottle, we went down to the bar, and there was a gang already in with the groom and his father-in-law to be. "Terry, Margaret, what're you having?" he asked.

I said, "We have just polished off a bottle of champers in the room."

"Only one; are you both sick?" He laughed, then gave Margaret a cuddle and kiss on the cheek. "So what're you going to have to drink, a couple of gins?"

"Yes please," Margaret replied and pecked him on the cheek. Off he went to the bar, coming back with two very large gins and one tonic, and we all chatted awhile before going into dinner.

I was up early the following morning, made some coffee, and took a cup in to Margaret. "I'm going to have a shower and get ready so I will be able to deal with anyone coming in for drinks."

"OK, Tel, but give me a kiss first," Margaret said. I obliged, and she had that saucy look in her eyes. "No," I said, and she poked out her tongue and said, "Spoilsport."

I'd just finished making the coffee when there was a knock on the door, it was the groom to have his hair trimmed. "You're early; come in and sit down, and Margaret will sort you out," I said.

While Margaret was trimming his hair, he asked if there was any chance of having a drop of bubbly. "OK," I said, "but I don't want you getting pissed before the wedding, as I will get the blame as best man."

He laughed and said he promised. When Margaret finished trimming his hair, he asked for another drink.

"When you have showered, dressed, and look lovely, yes. Then come back to have a drink."

"You're a very strict best man," he said, laughing. He left, and I looked at my Margaret and said, "Thank God for that."

She laughed and said, "I'm going for my bath." I started to finish getting dressed when there was a knock on the door. It was the waiter with a trolley full of sandwiches to be delivered to our room. "OK, bring it in," I said. After he left Margaret shouted from the bathroom, "Who was that?"

When I told her, she laughed and said I would be busy.

"Thanks a lot," was my answer, and then I thought, *Sod it*, and poured myself another drink. Five minutes later came a knock on the door, and in walked three exhibition blokes with their ladies and a chap we all called Big Bill.

"You going to be steward, Tel?" they asked.

"OK, help yourselves to the sandwiches, and I will pour you some bubbly." Once they started drinking and eating, Big Bill asked me, "Where's Margaret?"

"In the bath," I answered.

"Has she got a drink?"

"No."

He went to the bathroom door and shouted, "Margaret, do you want a glass of bubbly?"

Margaret shouted back, "Yes please!"

He looked at me, and I poured out a glass and gave it to him. He went to the door, knocked, and opened it, saying, "Here you go, darling."

Luckily Margaret had a bubble bath, and most of her was covered, except one breast, which was exposed as she took the drink. She thanked him, and he replied, "That's OK, your old man is a lousy barman." He came out, shut the door behind him, and asked for another drink.

Our room was like Liverpool street station, people coming and going up till eleven, when it was time to leave to the church. In the church, all went well. The bride looked beautiful, and as she looked up to the groom's eyes, I had to look away, for I know I would have had tears.

We all went back to the hotel, and the jazz band was half an hour late. But it was no problem; we sorted it out. Our demo was spot on. Everyone said it was fantastic, and one of the guests booked us to do a demo at their daughter's wedding.

After getting to bed about two in the morning, we were all at breakfast by nine, typical exhibition workers. After breakfast, the bride's dad asked me if we would take any bubbly back to our studio in London so he could have a drink when he comes down, no problem I said, good let's see if I can get the bar open, he did.

The next few weeks were nice and busy; also, one of the weekends we were at a ladies' night, making a nice break for us to get all dressed up, also to practise our dancing. I was progressing with my masonry, with the help of my Margaret, and next year would be going into the chair of my mother lodge.

The following weeks, we contacted all our friends, a couple of clients, and Mum and Dad to ask if they could make the wedding and how many wanted to stay the full weekend, as we had to book the Grand. The wedding was in two weeks' time. Finally, we got it all sorted, and Margaret rang the Grand.

When we finished work on Friday evening, Margaret came over and gave me a kiss. "What's that for?" I asked.

"Tel, this time next week, I will be your wife," she said with tears in her eyes.

"Don't cry, love," I said then kissed her.

"I'm so happy," she answered; then she really started to cry. With that, Ken came in from his room and asked what was the matter. I told him that Margaret was happy. "I would hate to see her when she's sad, then," he said, laughing.

"Come on," I said. "Let me lock up and we can all go for a drink."

Me and Margaret went to the studio on the Saturday morning to open the mail and to get a good start on the following week's work, as it was going to be a bit disrupted and hard to concentrate with our wedding that Friday. Even then, I couldn't get any sense out of my Margaret, for she was so excited. Every time I looked at her she got a little tearful when our eyes met.

"Tel?"

"Yes, love?" I answered.

"On Monday morning, can we go shopping to West Ken? I want to get a dress for Friday, but I don't want you to see it."

"Of course, love," I answered.

"What I will do is get a hat first; then you can go and get a tie to match it while I sort out a dress. Then we can meet at the perfume department after."

"OK, I will go along with that." I gave her a peck on the cheek. She still had watery eyes, so I made some coffee, and we carried on working till one, locked up the studio, and went for a drink.

On Monday, we went into the studio first, did a bit till eleven, then told Ken we were going shopping. Lucky for us, we found a parking meter about 50 yards from Barkers store, put in coins for two hours, as Margaret hated shopping and would be quick, and into the store we went, straight to the hat department. Within ten minutes, I was on my way to the gents' tie department, armed with a ladies hat, and Margaret went off to get a dress.

I found a dark tie with a nice flower embroidered on it, matching the hat. I paid for it and was off to the perfume department. As I was looking to see if they had any special offers, a hand slipped into mine from behind. I turned and got a kiss on the cheek.

"I can see you got your dress," I said.

"Yes, I know you will like it. I'm so excited!"

"Come on, let's go back to the studio before you get weepy again," I said.

"Alright, but while we are in the perfume department, I just want to get my attar for our wedding night, to go with opening the bubbly." She started to giggle.

"You're a naughty girl," I said.

"Yes, I know," she answered, still giggling. "That's why you love me so much."

"Fifth amendment."

We got back to the studio about two. Ken had some phone messages for us and gave them to Margaret; two were old clients and one was the gas council, calling to find out if we could do a mock-up of some houses, so they could set up some kind of gas leak for a competition. Margaret made an appointment for Tuesday week; it sounded interesting, like an outside film set.

The following days seemed to drag. We were busy, but they still seemed like long days. My best man rang up, and I made all the arrangements with him for Friday. On Thursday we finished at five thirty, then went for a drink before going home. After eating, we packed for Friday and went to bed early, as it was going an early start for us both the next day.

I was up at six, made some coffee, and took a cup up to Margaret, who was already sitting on the bed in her dressing gown. I passed the cup to her and asked if she was OK. She nodded and said she was still asleep. I got my cup then sat next to her. She smiled and said, "Tel, it's our day." She was weepy.

"Hey, come on. It's going to be a lovely day, and the sun is shining for us."

"I know, Tel. I will be alright when I have had a little kiss." I obliged.

Later, the best man arrived with his wife. She went upstairs to see Margaret, and I asked him if he would like a drink, as I was having one. He nodded, so I poured four glasses of bubbly and took two upstairs. I knocked on the door to ask if I could go in. Margaret said, "It's about time we had a drink," and she started to giggle.

"One of many today," I said, leaving them both giggling. Downstairs, I sat chatting with my best man, and we finished off the bottle. I shouted up, "See ya later, girls," and we left just after nine to the registrar's office, in my Scimitar with ribbons draped from it.

The office was only ten minutes away. We pulled in the car park and a lot of our guests were there. One of my mates bought out a hip flask. "Here, Tel, have a swig." I didn't want a second asking, as I was feeling a bit nervous.

Then, about ten to ten, my best man's wife arrived with my Margaret. Margaret got out of the car. God, she was so beautiful. I just looked at the wonderful lady I loved so much.

She came over to me, kissed me on the cheek, and said, "Tel, love, will I do?"

"Margaret, I just can't talk; you're so beautiful."

"There you go again, rose-coloured specks," she answered, and we went in.

The service was wonderful; the lady who did it was fantastic. It was like a church service. As we came out, the wife of one of my best clients came over to me and said, "Terry, that's the best day's work you have ever done." I have never forgotten those words, for the lady had been right.

After the photos were taken, we all headed off to Brighton. On arriving, everyone congratulated us. We checked in, the porter took our bags up to the suite, and we went into the bar to get a drink. In came all the guests to have a welcome drink before we went up to the suite. Then my best man said he was going up to set the cake up.

"What cake?" I asked.

"We have had a wedding cake made."

"That's so lovely of you," I answered. I went over and told my wife – yes, my *wife*. I was so proud. About fifteen minutes later, we all finished our drinks and up we went to the wonderful buffet the Grand had done. Also, there were six bottles of bubbly with the compliments of the Grand, and on a table on its own, a beautiful two-tier wedding cake. Everything was wonderful. I kissed my Margaret and said, "Happy darling?" She kissed me back and just said, "Tel."

The best man called everyone to order. He made a quick speech and said we should cut the cake before we reply, so we both went over to the cake. Margaret picked up the knife and tried to cut it. "Tel, you will have to help me, as the icing is hard to cut through," she whispered. So I put my hand over hers and pushed down. I just couldn't cut through.

After about three or four minutes, the best man said, "Hang on a minute." Everyone was laughing, and he came over, took off the top tier, lifted off the three supporting columns, and there was a bottle of pils lager in each column. Then he lifted off the base of the cake; it was iced 20mm blockboard with cans and bottles of pils lager under it. By this time, everyone, including us two, were in fits of laughter. The ladies' mascara was running, including my Margaret's, with tears of laughter.

Finally we all settled down, and I said, "How can we follow that?" I looked at Margaret; she was still giggling. I started to thank everyone for coming and making this wonderful for us, then Margaret chipped in, "and the well-baked cake." Everyone roared with laughter again. When they stopped, we said we hoped they all would enjoy the rest of the day and the weekend and thanked them again. The best man then said, "Can we kiss the bride now?"

"I thought you'd all done that downstairs in the bar," I answered.

"Yes, we did, but we all want another," he said.

"OK, but the groom wants one from the ladies." They all laughed.

At about five thirty, everyone went, and the two waitresses who had been looking after us said they would come back at eight and clear away so we could have a few hours' peace and quiet. We thanked them and collapsed on chairs, feeling a bit shattered after standing all day. I poured a couple of drinks, gave one to my Margaret, and sat back down. She looked at me and said, "What a day." I nodded and said, "What a cake." We both chuckled. "Tel, my love, I will remember this day for the rest of my life. I'm so happy." I got up, went over, and kissed her and said, "Me too, my lovely darling wife." We kissed again.

We got in the bar just after eight. We went and sat down with Mum, and Margaret ask if everything was OK. Mum said she and Dad were having a wonderful day. "You two were meant for each other, and you both look so happy," she said. We both said we were.

When we all went in to dinner, the staff had set a long table so we all could be together. After the meal, we were asked by the band leader to start the dancing. Everybody clapped, and we went over to the band. I shook their hands and Margaret kissed them, then we started to dance to more clapping. We were not joined by any other dancers till the next dance was played, and we came back shattered – two dances on the trot. The rest of the evening went well; everyone enjoyed themselves.

The band finished at midnight, and we went over and thanked them. This time, Margaret got the kisses. Some of the guests went to the bar for a nightcap, but others went up to their rooms, as did we.

There were still some full bottles and cans of pils left, which the staff had put in boxes for us. There was also half a bottle of bubbly, so I poured out a couple of glasses and gave one to Margaret, who was getting undressed. "Thanks, love," she said and gave me a quick peck and giggled. I had just started to get undressed when Margaret said, "I'll kill them." I looked over. Margaret had pulled back the bedclothes, and the bed was full of confetti. We both had to strip off the bedclothes and brush it all out. What a mess – confetti all over the carpet. Margaret giggled again and said, "Don't worry; be happy, Tel." Then I started to laugh. We remade the bed, drank our bubbly, then slipped into bed. Margaret snuggled up to me, and I kissed her tenderly and said, "Hallo, Mrs Parker." She whispered, "I love you, Tel. Love me."

I awoke at seven the following morning and looked across at my Margaret, who was still sleeping, thinking, *At last, my dreams have been answered. Margaret is now my lovely wife. I must be the luckiest bloke in the world.* I slipped out of bed, put my light dressing gown on quietly, then went over to make some coffee. I took a cup over and put it on the bedside table next to Margaret.

"Good morning, Mrs Parker," I said.

"Morning, darling," she answered.

"It's quite a nice day; the sun is shining," I said.

"I don't care if it's raining, Tel, as I have you to love me."

I bent over and kissed her. "Thank you, darling."

"More, please," she said, and I obliged.

About thirty minutes later, there was a knock on the door. I opened it, and there was a waiter with a trolley. "Mr Parker, good morning, with compliments of the manager." He wheeled in the trolley, I thanked him, and he left. Margaret came out of the bedroom, and I said, "It's our breakfast, with the manager's compliments."

"How sweet and kind of him," she said. On the trolley was a big bunch of flowers and a full English breakfast, toast, butter, fruit spreads, a jug of ice-cold orange juice, a bottle of bubbly, and a pot of coffee. I offered Margaret a chair at the table and said, "Would you like me to serve you, madam?"

"Ooh, yes please, darling." She giggled.

"Behave yourself, Mrs Parker," I said. My answer was another giggle and "No, I'm Mrs Parker now, so I can be naughty."

"What's new?" I replied, and I opened the bubbly. Then I realised what I had done. *Pop!* I looked at her. "Now who is thinking naughty things?" she said, giggling again.

"It makes a change for me to think naughty things," I answered.

"Now it's my turn to plead the Fifth Amendment." Margaret giggled. I made a couple of Buck's Fizzes, passed one to her, and winked. We ate our breakfast and finished off the bubbly and juice then went down to the hotel lounge, where we were greeted by some of our friends.

After about an hour, we decided to go out for a walk. It was really lovely outside; the sun was shining, the sea was calm, and there were no winds. We held hands and walked along the front, chatting and giggling, occasionally stopping and looking at the sea and having a cuddle. The rest of the weekend went marvellous; mind you, we both had rose-coloured specks. I just can't tell you how happy we both were – so in love with one another.

Sunday morning we said goodbye to all the staff at the hotel and all our friends and headed of back to London. Margaret asked, "Tel, when it comes to your ladies' night, can we have it at the Grand?"

"Darling, if the manager will give us a good deal, then yes, but we will be down there before then on weekend breaks and maybe a Christmas."

"Ooh, a Christmas sounds great, Tel!" Margaret squealed.

"I have the brochure," I said.

"Tel, you're a bugger, but a lovely one," she answered, giggling.

We got back home in time to have a couple of quick drinks in the pub at the bottom of the road, and the shellfish stall outside still had some fish left, so I got a couple of dressed crabs, a pint of large prawns and a pint of cooked mussels for our evening meal.

"Tel, you think of everything, darling," Margaret said.

"Yes, my love. Also, there are three bottles of bubbly in the fridge."

Margaret looked at me, giggled again, and said, "As I said before, Tel, you're a bugger."

We had a lazy afternoon dozing on the couch and had an early night after the long weekend. We cuddled up together and went to sleep.

I was in the studio early the following morning, as I wanted to do an hour on my Masonic ritual. I tried to do it every morning before I started work, but the last couple of days I hadn't. Then when Margaret came in, I could run through it with her, and she could correct me on my pronunciation. When Margaret came in, she was full of the joys of spring.

"Right, Tel, did you work on your ritual?" she asked.

"Yes, love," I answered.

"Right, let's hear it before I have a cup of coffee, as I want you to be perfect." Then she stopped being pushy, giggled, and said, "I want my ladies' night at the Grand."

"And you call me a crafty old bugger," I said. We both laughed, then I ran through the ritual.

"You're doing well, Tel, and getting better in remembering, even though you haven't done any over the weekend. Also, you're pronouncing your words better. I'm proud of you," she said, and she came over and gave me a kiss.

"Can we run through it again?" I said.

She laughed and said, "No, you get on with your work."

I poured out a couple cups of coffee, passed one over to Margaret, and checked on what I had to do.

We worked hard for the next couple of days. I was designing stands for later in the year, and Margaret was chasing up outstanding moneys owing and pricing designs that I had done. We were both pleased that we had the work, and I must say that we were very well organised now, thanks to my Margaret. Also, we were getting a very good name for our reliability, good service, and design; things were going great.

Then it was the day to go off to the gas council to find out what the outside job was all about. We got there a shade early – we liked to be early, never late. A nice lady showed us into a boardroom. About five minutes later, two middle-aged chaps came in. One of the men explained that it was a gas council competition; they were going to put porter cabins on a site, two side by side and one on top of the other. Our job was to design and make the cabins look like derelict houses, then they would put in a chemical that smelt like gas, then crews would be called in to find the leak. The fastest crew to find it would be the winner of the competition.

"We have asked three designers to submit designs and costings to undertake the whole job, so would you like to submit designs and costing?" he asked.

We said, "Yes, we would very much like to submit a design with full costing."

"That's good," one of the men replied, "and can you have it here by this time next week?"

"No problem," Margaret answered.

On getting back to the studio, Margaret told Ken, while I rang a Masonic friend of mine at the BBC to ask where I could buy false sheets of plastic bricks, slates, and such. He gave me a name of a company, and after lunch we went over to their works. The stuff they had would be just the job, so they gave me a thick brochure. In the car driving back, Margaret said, "You're quite excited about this job, aren't you, Tel?"

"Yes, love, it's a new challenge for me. Also, you, me, Ken, and a carpenter could do it without bringing in a contractor."

"Good thinking, Batman," Margaret said.

Ken was up for it, as I would pay him by the hour. Then I rang a freelance carpenter we used, told him all about it, and he was very keen. "That's it," I said, "I have had enough for today. The pub opens in ten minutes, so let's all go for a drink and have a chat about this job."

Off we went down to the pub at the bottom of the road, just as he opened. As we were talking about the gas job, I asked Ken if he knew where I could hire a flock spray.

"What do you want that for?" Margaret asked.

"Well," I said, "if we get the job, it would come in handy to spray false moss and rust, et cetera."

"Tel, you are really into this job."

"Yes, my love, I just can't wait till tomorrow when I get it on my board."

"I feel good about it, Tel," Margaret said. "You will get it because you're so confident; also, I know you, and you will put a lot of detail in your visual." She then looked at Ken and asked him what he thought. He said that he had never seen me so excited about a job before. He got up and said, "A couple more pils?" We both nodded.

While he was at the bar, my Margaret squeezed my hand, gave me a quick kiss, and said, "Tel, you're a lovely bloke, and I love you so much."

I kissed her back and told her she was a soppy old thing.

"Not so much of the old," she giggled.

Ken came back put the pils on the table and said that the firm who supplied the plastic brick panels would possibly know where I could get a flock spray. "Good thinking, Batman," Margaret said.

After about half an hour, Ken said he was off and would see us tomorrow. We had a couple of large gin and tonics, and then my Margaret said, "Tel, I have got to get home and get something out for dinner."

"Don't bother, love. We will eat out; I just fancy that."

"OK, Tel, you're on a high, so I will go along with that."

The following day, as expected I was in the studio early, put the coffee maker on, worked on my ritual for an hour, grabbed a second cup of coffee, and started to rough out the design for the gas council. Margaret came in about two hours later and asked how things were going.

"Well, I reckon by lunchtime, I will start to draw up a plan, elevation and visual, but I have got to check with the brochure on what bricks and slates to use."

"Good, I will tell anyone who rings that you're out and you'll ring them later, so you don't get interrupted."

"Thanks, love, I will give a kiss later."

"You had better."

I stopped for half an hour to eat a couple of rolls for lunch then worked through till six; all I had to do the following day was to colour in the visual. "That's it for today," I said.

Margaret came over and had a look. "Tel, that's really looking good," she said and kissed me on the cheek. "Thanks, love. Yes, it's coming on. Well, now let's lock up and have a quick drink before we go home."

"OK, love, the dinner has been on all day simmering. It's a casserole."

It was nearly seven when we got down the pub. I ordered two large gin and tonics. "Cheers, love," I said and took a big swig.

"You look shattered, Tel," Margaret said.

"I will be OK when I have had a couple of drinks, love," I answered, then I emptied my glass and got two more. We then sat chatting till eight, said good night to the landlord, and left.

On opening the front door, we were hit by the lovely smell of the dinner. "That makes me feel very hungry," I said. Margaret laughed and asked me to get the forks and spoons out. "OK, and I will pour out a couple of glasses of wine as well," I answered.

After we'd finished, I said to Margaret, "Dinner was smashing, just what I needed after a hard day's work."

"Is that all?" Margaret cheekily said.

"You're being naughty again," I replied.

"Yes, I know I am. Also I'm lovely too, so what are you going to do about it then, Tel?" she said, giggling.

"Well—"

Before I could finish, Margaret was on her way upstairs, calling out, "Leave the washing-up till tomorrow, Tel. And I could do with a drink – apart from other things."

I poured two drinks and took them up, and Margaret was already in bed. "Hurry up, Tel. It's cold; I forgot to put the blanket on."

"Margaret, it's summer. You don't need a blanket," I answered.

"Yes, I know, love, but I need you to keep me warm." I put Margaret's drink on her bedside table, had a sip of mine, then slipped into bed. Margaret pulled me to her. She was so soft. I gently put my arm round her and kissed her tenderly, and Margaret responded.

We both seemed to wake together the following morning, a little later than normal. I chucked my gown round me and went down to make the coffee. As I stood there waiting for it to finish, Margaret came in, put her arms round me and said, "Good morning, darling. Last night was fantastic. You must get excited about your drawings more often."

"Margaret, I don't need drawings," I answered.

"Tel, I'm only pulling your leg," she said, giggling.

"As that's the only thing you're pulling, it's OK," I answered.

"Now who is being naughty," she laughed.

About an hour later, I was in the studio. Ken was already there and had made the coffee. After I finished off the visual, I called Margaret over to look at it. "Tel," she said, "that's looks great, but now we have to cost it, so I will ring the carpenter to see if he can pop in tomorrow. In the meanwhile, you work out how much plastic fabricating it will need. After I have spoken to the chippy, you check how much a flock spray will cost to hire."

While Margaret was on the phone, I went in, showed Ken the drawings, and said that when the chippy comes in, we would all sit down and work out the hours involved. With that, Margaret came in telling us that the chippy would be here at nine in the morning. "Also, Tel," she said, "I have made an appointment to see the client at ten Thursday morning. He was pleased that we had a design to show him, and we were the first to contact him."

"Good," I said, "it makes us look on the ball."

I got a price to hire the flock spray machine and some flock, gave it to Margaret, then started to make my presentation folder. As I was putting the finishing touches to it, Ken said, "See ya tomorrow," and left. I looked at my watch. "God, Margaret," I said, "it's nearly seven."

"Don't worry, darling," she said, "I got some fish out of the freezer this morning, so it won't take long to get the dinner ready."

We left just after seven and went straight home. I poured a couple glasses of wine while Margaret got the dinner ready. After dinner, we sat watching telly and Margaret said, "I think we have a good chance of getting this job, as you have done a wonderful design. It looks so good."

"We will see, my love. I just don't know what the other designers will submit. They might be film set designers and know more about outside sets than I do."

Margaret snuggled up to me, kissed me on the cheek, and said, "Tel, I have just got a feeling about this. When the client said we were the first to make an appointment with a design, he seemed to be impressed."

"Let's hope so, my love," I answered and poured another couple of drinks. We sat quietly for a while, sipping our drinks. Then Margaret said, "Let's have an early night, as we have an early start tomorrow."

I agreed and said, "You go up; I will bring up a couple of drinks."

We were both in the studio early. Ken was already there and had made the coffee. We had just started to drink, and the chippy turned up. Margaret gave him a coffee. We all sat down to have our meeting. We worked out what materials were needed, and I explained how the roof sections would be made for a quick assembly and that I would produce all work drawings that would be needed. We finished at midday, and the chippy wished us luck with our presentation then left.

Right back to the drawing board I went, to get on with other work I had to do. Margaret called across, "Tel, you haven't done any ritual yet today, so do an hour before you start."

"OK love," I answered. She came over gave me another cup of coffee, kissed me on the cheek, and said, "Good boy, you have got your little book out." She smiled and went back to her desk.

Ken left about four, as he had some poly to fix on a couple of stands in Olympia, and said he would see us in the pub about seven. We worked on till six thirty. The pub was quite busy, but we managed to find a table. Margaret sat down, and I went and got three pils, one for Ken when he arrived. Halfway through our drinks, Ken came in and joined us. We asked if all went well, and he said, "Yes, but I have got a couple of extras to cut and fix tomorrow."

"Good, more work," Margaret said. We all laughed.

Thursday came at last. We were up very early and went round to the studio together. Margaret put on the coffee while I sorted out my presentation. As we were drinking our coffee, Ken walked in, as he had some extra poly to cut and then fix. "There must be an easier way of earning a living," he laughingly said.

"Yes," Margaret answered, "but not as much challenge or satisfaction from the result; yes, we have a lot of pressure and problems, but we also have a lot of fun. It's a great life, very similar to show biz."

We both agreed. Ken went into his room and Margaret said to me, "You have half an hour to read your book."

"Bully," I answered.

"You will thank me when you're in the chair next month, as I want all the lodge to look up to you as a good master, Tel, and I know you won't let me down. Like your work, you put all your heart into it." I went over and kissed her. "Come on, there is no time for that now – get on that book."

After half an hour, I said, "Come on, we had better get going." I said ciao to Ken and off we went to the gas council. We were five minutes early but were shown straight up to the little boardroom. As we arrived, the two gents came in, followed by a cracking young lady with coffee. We all sat and had a little chat while drinking the coffee, then I showed them my design and Margaret gave them the price. I ran through a couple of things on the design with them, then waited for their comments. They didn't say anything for about three to four minutes. Then they said they were very impressed and would let us know their answer after they had seen the other designs and showed them to their bosses, but it would be by five this evening.

In the car, I asked Margaret what she thought of our chances. "Tel, my lovely darling, I think they are very good, and tonight we will be celebrating."

"Margaret, if you're right, we will be off to the Grand this weekend for a bargain break."

We got back to the studio, had a bit of lunch, then started work. I kept looking at the clock; it didn't seem to move. It was just after four, and the phone rang. It was one of the toy companies I did stands for, wanting us to go and see them regarding next year's show. Margaret made a quick appointment and hung up.

I got a cup of coffee and asked Margaret if she would like one. She nodded. "I just can't do any more work," I said. The waiting was getting to me.

Margaret giggled and said, "Tel, don't worry; be happy." I just smiled.

The phone went again. It was a contractor who had a query on a stand he was building for us. I had a quick chat with him, sorted it out, and hung up. It was now nearly five, I looked at my Margaret and said that it didn't look like we got it. I had just finished and the phone went again. Margaret picked it up, looked at me, and nodded. "It's the gas council, Tel. They want to speak to you."

I picked up my extension and feebly said hallo.

"Hi, Terry. I'm pleased to tell you that the contract is yours."

"Thank you very much," I answered, as I gave Margaret the thumbs up. He went on to say that the three designs were all good, but what swung it for us was the imprint of a dirty football on the house wall, such detail. I laughed and said, "A little thing like that?"

"Yes, Terry, a little thing like that." He said he would speak to us next week to give us all the details.

I put down the phone. Margaret came flying over to me and gave me a big smacker then said, "I told you we would get it." Then she kissed me again before I could answer. I told her about the football print on the wall of the house. She laughed, kissed me again, and said, "I will book the Grand now, as Mr and Mrs Parker for real." I laughed, then she said, "This is a big feather in our cap. I love you."

"Ditto, my love."

The following morning, we told Ken, and I rang the chippy to give him the good news. We had already worked out the materials, so my Margaret ordered everything we needed and I hired a flock spray machine and ordered some green and brown flock. Then I went round to the dyeline printers and got six copies of my working drawings. I looked at Margaret and said, "I think we have covered everything."

She nodded. I poured a couple of cups of coffee, passed one to Margaret, and sat on the chair in front of her desk. She looked at me and said, "Tel, love, I just can't believe it; you must be very proud of yourself in getting this job. I have always told you that you're brilliant."

"Margaret, my lovely lady, it's down to you, for your love, support, and help, you have given me the confidence I badly needed."

Margaret then came round from her desk, put her arms round me, kissed me tenderly, and said, "Tel, you are a very clever man. You're a brilliant artist and designer, helpful and dedicated, giving a hundred per cent to every job you undertake, and on top of this, you're a lovely kind loving man." She kissed me again.

I then said "Can I have a rise then?"

"I will think about it in the Grand." She giggled.

As usual we were well received at the Grand and had a lovely break, but it went too quickly. Before leaving, we had a chat with the manager about a special rate for my ladies' night later in the year. He said that he would work out a good price and send it to us later the following week.

The next week or so was normal. The gas council job was all made and ready for us to put together on site in a couple of weeks' time. We were all praying that the weather would be good. Then on Monday, a week before we were due to set it all up, we had a phone call from a girlfriend of my daughter Terrie. She asked if she could bring Terrie up to see us, as she was having big problems in her marriage. "Of course," I said.

"I will bring her up tomorrow."

I gave her directions for how to get to us and said, "We will see you then." I put the phone down, and Margaret asked, "What was that all about, Tel?" I told her what Terrie's friend had said. "It don't sound too good, love, does it?" Margaret replied.

"No, it don't, love."

The following day, we were both in early so we could get most of our work done before the girls came up. Margaret was very nervous, as she had never met any of my kids. I told her, "Don't worry; be happy." She smile and told me to get my own sayings, but I could see she was worried.

Just before twelve, the girls walked in. I went over and kissed them both, then introduced my Margaret. Margaret shook their hands, kissed them both on the cheek, and offered them both some coffee. Terrie was watching Margaret's every move. I gave them chance to settle, then I said, "Now what's this all about? And I won't mince my words, but Terrie, you look rough."

Margaret said, "Tel, steady, can't you see Terrie is not well?"

Terrie said it was OK; she knew that she looked rough, and then her friend stepped in and said, "Terrie's husband has been knocking her about. Show them, Terrie."

Terrie then took off her coat. Her arms were all bruised. Then she undid the top of her blouse and pulled it over to expose her shoulder. This also was very badly bruised. Margaret looked shocked. "Terrie, you poor young lady, how long as it been going on for?"

"Quite a while," Terrie answered, and she started to cry. Margaret went across and put her arms round her. "Tel, get the brandy from the cupboard and put some in Terrie's coffee."

I got the brandy put a good shot in the coffee and gave it to her. She sipped it while Margaret still comforted her. Terrie's friend looked at me and told me that it had been going on for a long time. "Why the hell didn't she get in touch with me?" I asked her.

"She was frightened of what you might say."

I looked at her and said, "Just because I'm divorced, it doesn't mean that I don't love my kids. And my Terrie – I just can't tell you how much I miss and love her. She used to go everywhere with me, and when I first started on my own she helped me with the books. It's so sad to see this has happened to her."

"I know, Terry. I remember when I used to stay at your house. That's why I rang you," she answered.

Terrie was now getting better. She looked at Margaret and said, "You're a very kind lady, and I can see why my dad loves you."

Margaret said, "I will make some more coffee." She took the jug out to our little kitchen to get some water. But I knew my Margaret; she went out there to have a weep. I looked at Terrie and asked if she was feeling better. She nodded. Margaret came back with a jug of water. I asked her if she was OK; she smiled and nodded, knowing that I knew she had been weeping.

"Right now, my lovely lady," I said to Terrie, "you're going to have to get a divorce."

She nodded and said, "Yes, but it takes a long time."

"Terrie, leave it to me. I will have a chat with my solicitor, as I'm sure this will go through quickly, for he has been beating you. But you will have to leave him and see if you can live with your mother for a short while till you can get sorted out."

Margaret said, "Tel, it's a pity we are so far away, as Terrie could live at home with us."

Terrie looked at me and said, "Dad, your Margaret is so understanding. I wish Mum was like that."

"Terrie, shhhh, your mum just don't understand a lot of things, but that's her way," I answered.

We sat for about another hour, chatting about what might happen, then the girls said they were going before the roads got too busy. Terrie got up and went straight over to Margaret, kissed her, thanked her, and said, "There's no need for me to say look after my dad, because I can see you both love one another so much." She then came over to me, kissed me, and said "You're a lucky man, Dad, as you have a lovely lady." I thanked her and said I would be in touch but she would have to let me know where she would be.

Margaret flopped in her chair, looked at me, and said, "Tel, I could do with a shot of that brandy in my coffee." I obliged. I needed one too. Margaret sipped her coffee and said, "That's nice." Then she looked at me. "That poor girl – to be knocked about like that, it's criminal. Tel, she's a lovely young lady. You must be so proud of her."

I nodded, but I had tears in my eyes, for the shock of seeing here bashed about like that was just registering. Margaret spotted this, came over, and put her arms round me. "Tel, she said things will be alright, you'll see. Please try not to upset yourself."

I gave her a kiss and thanked her for being so kind to her.

"Tel, she is a lovely girl, and she is my daughter now." She then kissed me.

"Yes, I suppose she is," I answered. We finished our special coffees and shouted through to Ken that we were going home. We asked him to lock up and went straight home after a very stressful day.

Indoors, Margaret said, "You sit down. I will get you a large gin and tonic."

I thanked her and asked, "What about you?"

"What do you think?"

I flopped on the couch. Margaret came over with two glasses, one for me, and the other for her. She sat down, and we both sipped at our drinks. I said, "I don't want many more days like that."

The next month went past quite quickly. We did the gas job, and the client was well pleased. A contractor that we had done designs for folded, owing us £1200, we went to the creditors' meeting, but there was no chance of getting any of it back. I became Worshipful Master of my lodge. Work was a little slow coming in, but it was still coming in, so we had something to do every day.

The end of next month was my ladies' night, so we went out to get a nice dress. We looked at quite a few, then my Margaret tried on a beautiful white dress. She looked gorgeous; it was just her, the style was like what Cleopatra the queen of Egypt wore in the film. "Don't bother to look at any others, my love, for that's the one. You look a million dollars in it."

She smiled, thanked me with a kiss, and said it felt good on. After paying for it, Margaret said, "While we are in the store, I must go and get my nightdress." So over to the perfume department we went for her Calvin Klein perfume. "Shall we get a bottle of bubbly?" I laughingly said. Margaret giggled and told me to behave myself.

The ladies' night went great; the Grand was at its best, with the food and service, and my Margaret looked stunning and so beautiful. I can see her now. The hotel had matched the pink menus I had designed with pink serviettes and pink flowers on the tables, but the best was to come with the cabaret we had booked. We had seen these chaps at a previous ladies' night we'd gone to and there wasn't a dry eye in the house once they had started, so we managed to find and book them for ours.

"Right, I will start." The manager of the group went on the stage, took the mike, and said, "Ladies and gentlemen." As he said this, the lights were slightly dimmed. He then went on, "For your entertainment tonight," he paused, then he shouted, "the bannerettes!"

"YMCA" was loudly played, the doors of the hall burst open, the lights went up, and in came thirty blokes of all different sizes, dressed in miniskirts, fishnet tights, turned-down Wellington boots, T-shirts with a big sash draping over their shoulders, lettered "bannerettes", full-face crash helmets, and American rah-rah girls sticks, marching to the song all in routine.

There were howls. Ladies were crying. I just can't explain how funny it was, and it got even better. As they finished, the leader came over to my Margaret and offered her a go – but to his surprise, Margaret said OK. She pulled up her dress between her legs and sort of tucked in her knickers, kicked off her size-3 dance shoes, put on these great big Wellington boots and crash helmet, and took the rah-rah stick. She lined up with the blokes, the music started, and off she went. Because Margaret is so little, her being dressed like that, with big boots and crash helmet, just brought the house down.

They did a shortened version of the routine, and when it was finished Margaret sat, kicked off the boots, and took off the helmet. Her hair was all wet from sweat and her mascara had all run down her cheeks. She then stood up to untuck her dress and put on her shoes, and everybody clapped. The leader of the group told me that it was the first time a lady had taken up the challenge since they had started. I just said, "That's my Margaret."

I went over, kissed her, and said, "Well done."

She kissed me back and said, "It was bloody hot under that helmet. I must have a drink before I go and fix my face and hair."

I gave her a cold glass of lager. After Margaret had finished the drink, she said, "Won't be long. I'm going to tidy myself up and put my face back on."

"OK," I said, and I whispered in her ear, "I love you." She giggled and went off, which left me thinking what a wonderful lady I have.

Margaret was soon back, looking as lovely as ever. She grabbed me, gave a quick kiss, and said, "Come on, Tel, let's give this dance floor some stick."

"Right love, they're playing a jive. Let's show them how to do it." So we went into our routine: start clapping, about 20 yards apart, then do little steps, meet each other, and start to jive. We were first on the dance floor, and it stayed that way till the end of the dance, when everybody clapped and one of the lodge members shouted, "Great, another cabaret!" We both laughed and said thanks to all.

We both got into work early Monday morning. I made the coffee while Margaret checked the answer machine, as there was a message on it. "Good God," she said, "do you know who that was, Tel?"

"No, love," I answered.

"It was the chairman of one of the biggest toy groups in the country, and he wants to see us regarding designing his group's stand at the next toy fair in London!"

I just looked at her in amazement. "You sure?" I said.

"Yes, love, I met him when I was at the design council. He is a big, tall, nice chap. Tel, if we can get this job, it will be fantastic."

"We will do our best, love," I said.

"OK, love, you're the designer, and I'm the charmer," she answered, giggling. Later that day, Margaret made an appointment for us to see him the following morning at his office in Oxford Street.

We arrived at the offices fifteen minutes early, went straight in to the reception, and told the young lady behind the desk who we were. "Yes," she said, "I have a note that you would be coming this morning. Would you take a seat? I will let him know you're here."

About five minutes later, this very tall man came out of the lift. We both stood up. He went to Margaret first, shook her hand, and said, "I have met you before at the design council; you're Margaret Ensbury."

Margaret laughed and answered, "Yes, you have met me before, but I'm now Margaret Parker."

He laughed, looked at me, shook my hand, and said, "And you're the lucky husband, Terry Parker."

"Yes," I said, "very lucky."

He laughed again and said, "Let's go upstairs, and I will get some coffee laid on." He showed us into a boardroom, ordered the coffee, then came and sat with us. After a young lady brought in the hot coffee, he said, "We have booked a very big area in the London toy fair. I'm told that you have a lot of clients you design and build stands for in this show, and you're very reliable and practical. Now, what we are looking for is a system to bring the five companies under one roof that looks good. Do you think you can come up with something like this?"

Margaret looked at him and said, "Terry did it for me when I was at the design council, so I can't see any problem."

"Yes, I saw that and was very impressed," he said.

"I'm sure that I can do something like that, but a lot more exiting, as it's for toys, for you. Once I see your area and floor plan, I will work out a design," I answered.

"That's great, Terry. The organizer said you're the best chap to ask," he said smiling.

Then Margaret chipped in and said, "Yes, it worked for me, then I ended marrying him."

On the way home in the taxi we chatted about what had happened and what a big feather in our caps it would be if we landed this contract. "Tel," Margaret said, "I know this man; he wouldn't ask us if he hadn't checked us out first. So I'm sure that if you come up with a good idea that is practical, we will be home and dry."

"Darling, the little grey cells are already working," I answered.

"I thought they might," Margaret said as she leant over and kissed me on the cheek.

"More, please," I said.

"Later, darling, later," Margaret whispered.

I worked out a complete panel system which was based on my system that didn't use poles, but it was a lot more fancy. It was clad in a suede, with a good polished wooden frame around and gold-faced, raised letters on each panel. There were 186 panels, 1 metre wide; also, every 3 metres there were window bays to conform with the regulations; they allowed the companies to display their product, and of course, there were fire exits and five large main entrances for the different companies to have a stand built within. It was some massive operation. After I had done the block plan and elevation and the coloured visual I called Margaret over to my drawing board to have a look.

"Tel, it looks wonderful. It's one hell of a job to cost," Margaret said.

"That's down to you, my love," I answered.

"Thanks a lot," was her reply. It was my turn now to laugh, and I did, saying that I was just going round to get the dyeline prints so we could get them in the post tonight to the contractors. "I'll sort you out when you come back," she said, giggling.

We got the group stand and one of the group's interiors, but what a toy fair this turned out to be – we had twelve other stands as well as the big group's one. We were working flat out, getting everything done.

We also had three stands in the Harrogate toy fair, a couple of weeks before the London one, but everything was ready to go a week before we went to Harrogate. But there were rumours of a road and transport strike; this would mean that the boats in Earls Court wouldn't be lifted out of the large pool, and the toy fair follows the boat show – big worries. Everyone to do with the trade was worried because if they couldn't lift the boats out, the pool couldn't be emptied, and the ground floor couldn't be used.

We were up in Harrogate when we were told the strike was on. As soon as we got back to London, I rang the London toy organizer. He told me there was a meeting in a couple of days, and all designers, contractors, and exhibitors who would be affected by this would be informed. All the companies that had stands on the ground floor of Earls Court would be transferred to Olympia; the stands upstairs would stay. He handed out the new layouts – it sounded easy, but five of our stands were switched to Olympia, including the big group, and of course, the areas had changed, so it was back to the drawing board. But there were more problems, as most of the stands were made. We did a thirty-hour shift, only stopping to eat and drink. Margaret even set up a little camping cooker in the studio so we could have hot food to keep us going.

We'd done it. Margaret rang the contractors to come and collect the revised drawings, which they did and thanked us. We were a really shattered and not looking forward to the build up, being in two different halls, a long way apart. I told Margaret that we would have to split up; while I was at Earls Court, she would have to be at Olympia. Then at lunchtime we would change round, but it was going to be very hard getting any extras done on site.

The weather was wicked all through the build up period. We were working till ten every night, seeing clients at their hotels, ringing contractors at all different hours, night and day, but the stands were all finished and ready on time. The clients were very happy and all told us that we were fantastic to get every finished and ready with all the problems we had.

We went home and had a quick drink. It was now well past five. I looked at Margaret, and she nodded, smiled, and went up to pack. I picked up the phone to book, and a half-hour later, we were on the road to the Grand.

The following months trundled on with the usual problems associated with the exhibition trade, and more companies were exhibiting at the NEC Birmingham, so Margaret and I were thinking of moving, maybe in Bucks border, between London and Birmingham.

On one of our visits to my mum and dad, we told them what we were thinking on doing. They said if we got a big house, they'd sell theirs and put their money in with ours, and we could all live together. It sounded a good idea, so we said that we would have a couple of days off in a couple of weeks' time and have a look round.

The following week, we had to go and see an old client to take a briefing for a stand at the NEC. He asked how we were, and I said, "OK, but fed up with having to drive up to the NEC, so we are going to look for a big house in Bucks."

He told us that he was selling his big house in Silverstone Village Northants, and it was about 10 miles between the M1 and the M40.

What a bit of luck! We told him we would get in touch with Mum and Dad, then give him a ring to come up to see it.

On the way back, Margaret said to tell them they could stay with us for a couple of days. I rang them as soon as we were back to the studio. They were pleased and said they would drive up to us the following day. Mum and Dad arrived safely, and the following day we set off to see the house in Silverstone. We found it without any problem, drove up the side drive, and parked in front of a massive garage. A very pleasant lady answered the door and told us she was his wife. She invited us in and showed us into the lounge.

What a place this was! Dad sat down in a big armchair and said, "I will stay here till we move in."

Mum said, "You haven't seen the house yet."

"I don't have to," he said. "This is just a wonderful place." We all agreed.

My client's wife then returned with coffee and asked if we would like to have a look round while the coffee cooled. We all agreed.

The house was a four-hundred-year-old cottage with an extension built attached to it (this could well be a separate living area). The whole place was massive, standing on a lot of land. Upstairs, there were six very large bedrooms and two big bathrooms. Best of all, one of the bedrooms had a big glass sloping window in the roof giving a Northern light, perfect for an artist. I looked at my Margaret. She squeezed my hand, smiled, and said, "Tel, this is marvellous. It will make a great studio."

We then went downstairs. The extension had a large room with a private entrance and a very large room at the side of it. Dad said the smaller room could be their kitchen and dining room, and the other room could be their lounge if that was OK with us. We both nodded.

There was also a little toilet under the stairs, then a large kitchen with a boiler room, a dining room with a cellar under, a very large lounge with a inglenook fireplace and wood burner, and at the end of the lounge was a door leading to a large wash- or workroom. It just was unbelievable. We all looked at each other and nodded, so I put in an offer, thanked my client's wife, and we left. On the way home, there was one topic of conversation: the cottage and how wonderful it was.

It was about eleven the following morning we got a phone call in the studio from our client; the offer had been accepted. We still had some bottles of bubbly from the wedding, so I opened one, got the usual giggle from my lovely Margaret, and had a drink just as Mum and Dad came in from shopping.

Margaret shouted, "Mum, Dad, we got it!"

Silly cow, she was crying. I poured a couple of glasses for them, but a very small one for Mum, as she didn't drink. We all said cheers and drank our bubbly. Mum made a face but drank a drop, and Margaret came over, kissed Mum and Dad, then kissed me hard, and after, she whispered, "Good night, darling."

Mum and Dad sold their house very quickly. I applied for a £20 thousand mortgage and was accepted, but the sale of Margaret's house fell through at the last minute, as the buyer couldn't raise the deposit, so we had to take out a bridging loan. This was very bad news, for the interest was very high. But we wanted the house, so we signed up and moved in.

Then, to make matters worse, my middle daughter, Debbie, told us she was going to get married and wanted us to pay out a lot of money towards the wedding they had arranged. We told her we just couldn't come up with that type of money, as we were on a bridging loan. Knowing she worked in a bank, we believed she would understand, but she wouldn't accept this and said we wouldn't be welcome at the wedding. This really hurt me. My Margaret tried to comfort me, but it was one of the saddest times in my life – and I have had a fair share. The day she married, I sat up in my studio, crying nearly all day. It was hard for Margaret to see me like this, but she did help with her love and cuddles.

Apart from working all day, back to the bar I went for extra cash some evenings and weekends at the local pub. I hated it but it had to be done. We also started to make wines, following Dad's footsteps, because money was tight, but it was also it was good fun going out and picking the different wild fruits. The wine was quite strong to say the least. After a couple of years, when locals had sampled our wines, it was said, "If you go to Pyghtle Cottage, don't drink the wine!" We had a hell of a reputation for lovely, clear, good, and very strong wine.

One sunny Saturday afternoon there was a cricket match down the village club, so we went down with a few sandwiches and a gallon container with our homemade wine and some plastic glasses. One of the older players was enjoying our wine. It came time for him to go in to bat, but first ball, he was out. When he came back, Margaret said to him, "Didn't you see the ball?"

"Margaret, I didn't see the F-ing bowler," he answered. Then he asked if we had any wine left.

"No problem," we said, and we gave him another, laughing.

After about six months, we got a phone call. Margaret's house was sold, and the money was being transferred. What great news! At last we could start earning some money for our company and not for the bank, so we celebrated with some homemade wine.

About a month after moving in, we came back from shopping and Mum said she had a phone call about a bed and breakfast. The callers said they had stayed here before, as it used to be a guest house. Mum said she would ring them back after she had checked with us. "Yes," I said, remembering what the lady had told us. Margaret immediately said, "Go for it, girl! It will be a bit more pension for you both." She started giggling and then said, "You might get some good-looking blokes."

So now Mum was in the hotel business, and we were getting plenty of work, including small graphics from local little companies. Also, we were going to quite a few ladies' nights. We took Terrieand our friends from Birmingham who had been at our wedding to one in Welwyn Garden City, and what a laugh! To start off, I picked the hotel, as it was just across from the venue where the function was, but it was like Fawlty Towers, and we were glad we weren't eating in there that evening. Yet we all had a great night and, as usual, got our drinks by the bottles, so at the end we got a cardboard box and took what was left back to the hotel for nightcaps.

We had a bit of trouble getting back into the hotel, as the night porter was asleep, but after about ten minutes, we managed to wake him and he let us in. We went straight into the lounge, and my Margaret asked him if he would like a drink. He nodded and said, "Please."

"Good," she said, "so if you get some glasses, we all can have a drink." Off he went, and within minutes he was back with a tray of glasses. I asked if there was any chance of some cheese and biscuits, and off he went again, a little wobbly from the drink. Ten minutes later, back he came with a big plate of cheese, crisps, nuts, and biscuits. We gave him another drink, and we all carried on drinking and chatting for about another hour and decided to call it a day. The porter was now sound asleep again.

In our room, Margaret said, "Tel, we have had a wonderful time with some lovely friends." I agreed, and we cuddled up to each other in bed, kissed, and this time went to sleep.

The following morning was quite funny to some. I woke about seven, gasping for a drink. A beer would have been marvellous, as coffee would be no good, but I had a drop of gin left and a bottle of tonic and a fridge in the room with some ice in it. That would do, so I filled the bath, made a gin ice and tonic, slipped into the bath and sipped my drink.

Margaret woke and called, "Where are you, Tel?"

I answered, "In the bath having a drink."

"OK, what are you drinking?"

"Gin, any left?"

"No, only Scotch." Then in she came, holding a Scotch and ice. "Move up, I want to get in."

I did, and we sat there talking and drinking. There was a knock on the door. "Come in," I shouted.

It was Terrie. She came in and saw us silly old buggers in the bath drinking and chatting.

"I'm sorry," she said.

Margaret said, "No problem, do you want a drink?"

"God, no," Terrie said. "I just want to know if I can have your milk, as you drink black coffee."

Margaret said, "You can have the coffee too, if you want it, as me and old Tel have a better morning drink." She giggled. Terrie smiled and thanked us, but I know she thought we were both barmy.

Maybe we were barmy, but we were barmy together.

When we got down to breakfast, it was like a music hall. The breakfasts that were ordered came up different; then, if there was a sausage missing from one of the plates, the waiter went over and used a fork to take one off a plate that had already been given to one of the guests and put it onto the plate that was missing one. It was so mad, we just sat and giggled while we were eating. In all the hotels we had stayed in, we had never seen anything like this before.

I must give you a laugh about an exhibition we did up in Stonehaven, Scotland. We had a modular system that we hired out to a well-known company who manufactured soap, toothpaste, and disposable nappies. About every three to four months, we would take the system and product to small nurse and midwife shows all over the UK.

For this exhibition, we left with a hired box van, two days early, staying halfway up in a travel lodge. We got to Stonehaven early and found the hall OK. It was an old building, and the show was going to be upstairs. I looked at Margaret and said, "Bloody lot of lumping to do."

She giggled, saying, "Don't worry; be happy." We couldn't set up till 2 p.m. The show opened at 5 p.m. and it finished at 9, so Margaret chatted up a parking warden to reserve us a place right outside of the entrance, promising him some product. He agreed, so off we went to book a room for the night. This was easier said than done, for every hotel we went to was fully booked because of the show. Time was running out, so I drove back to the hall to get unloaded. The parking bloke was on the ball, as he had put down some cones. It was ten to two, but they said it was OK for us to start. I opened the back of the van and helped Margaret to get in. The first thing she did was to get out some products to give to the warden. He was well pleased and said we could park there as long as we wanted.

After about an hour, everything was unloaded and upstairs. I was shattered. I said to Margaret, "There is a pub next door; let's go in for half an hour and have a drink and rest before we set the stand up."

Margaret nodded and said, "I never thought you would ask," and giggled. I ordered a pint and a half of lager. God, it was good, lovely and cold. The landlord asked if we were next door with the show, and Margaret told him what we were doing. As I ordered another, Margaret told the landlord about the problem we were having to get somewhere to stay. He said, "I do bed and breakfast; I have a room if you want it."

I looked at Margaret; she just couldn't stop laughing. We had been driving round for hours to find somewhere to stay, and there was a place right next door. Margaret asked if she could see the room, so the landlord took her up, and a couple of minutes later, they came down and Margaret said she had booked. Also, he said he could do a late meal for us, if we liked steak, so Margaret booked that as well. "You're a darling," I said and kissed her.

We finished our drinks and went back to the hall to set up the stand. While we were setting up, I asked Margaret what the room was like. It's OK, love. Small, with a shower, but the toilet is outside, across the passage."

I told her, "I'm not worried about the toilet, but I'm glad it has a shower." She started to giggle again. "What's so funny?" I asked.

"Nothing," she said, and she kept giggling.

Once it was all set up, we handed it over to the rep and told him we would see him about 8.30 and left. We went into the pub and had a drink and then went up to the room. As I was unpacking, I said that I would have a quick shower. Margaret started to giggle again.

"Now what's the matter?" I asked.

"Nothing," she answered, still giggling.

I thought, *Silly cow*, then I asked, "Where's the shower room?" Now she was killing herself with laughter. She pointed to a cupboard. I went over and opened it, and as I did, a base tray dropped down, a top frame swung round with a curtain, and there was the shower unit, small, but a shower. I looked at Margaret, and she was still laughing. "Good luck, darling."

I answered, "No problem." I stripped then said, "Sorry, my love, the shower is too small; you can't join me."

"OK Tel, but I can dry you off after," she said, giggling.

"But we haven't any bubbly," I answered.

"You're a bugger."

Also while we were north of the border, we had a stand that I designed in Glasgow. We had to oversee the build up in the new Glasgow exhibition halls. We arrived at our hotel on the outskirts about midday. After unpacking, we went down to the bar, but it was closed as it was being redecorated. We were told that there would be a temporary bar set up in the dining room in the evening. We asked if there was a decent pub nearby and were told there was a private club just round the side of the hotel. We found it with no trouble, and – what a bit of luck – there was a big Masonic sign up over the entrance. In we went, and a nice gent came over and asked if he could help. I told him who I was, and he checked me out then greeted us well and took us in, introducing us to the staff and about ten customers, and bought us a drink. We sat there chatting to everyone and had a couple of sandwiches. The bar was doing a special offer on Canadian club whisky, a large measure for the price of a single. The jocks didn't drink it, but we did.

Suddenly, in came a load of noisy blokes. Then they stopped making a noise and looked at us; everything went quiet. The gent we first met got up, went over to them, and said we were just visitors from London working up here. Then they all started to chat again. As the gent came back over to us, I started to laugh, realising what the problem was: all the blokes were in blue, Rangers supporters, but my lovely Margaret had a green-and-white top on, Celtic colours. He said the club was also the Rangers supporters club. So Margaret stood up and cheekily shouted out to the supporters, "I will take it off if it upsets you lads." They all cheered, and some came over and gave her a kiss and shook my hand. One asked Margaret if she would have really taken off her top.

"Of course, I wouldn't want to upset you chaps, and I do have a bra on underneath."

"You're, great sports, you two, and the club would like to invite you both to our dance tonight." We accepted and had a great night.

As the months passed by, we were getting a bit concerned about the computer. Yes, we had one that Margaret used, and I used it for typesetting but I really didn't like what was going on. Clients could now do their own graphic artwork, and in some cases, line drawings and signs, so we were getting very little graphic work. We carried on doing well on the exhibitions, but again, we could see that exhibition design was also being done on the computer. Then a big shock – right in the middle of the toy fair build up in London, my mum had a heart attack.

The computer taking away a lot of work, and now we had to keep an eye on Dad; things were not looking roses. There was the bed and breakfast that Mum used to do, so we decided to do bed and breakfast, but more than Mum did. Also, we would do home-cooked evening meals with free homemade wine.

So now we were in the hotel business. After about six months, I cashed in a big pension I had and stopped trading as an exhibition designer. It was a very sad day for us, after all the hard work we had put into the company, designing stands and overseeing them in every city in the UK, plus going to France and Switzerland, a bloody computer could put skilful people out of business.

My Margaret cuddled up to me, gave me a kiss on the cheek, and said, "Tel, my lovely darling, we still have one another, and remember what I always say…"

"Don't worry; be happy," we said together, then kissed.

We carried on doing the bed and breakfast and got well-known for our good food. As folks checked out, they checked in for the following year, and many became very dear friends. On one of the GP weekends, four lads who had stayed with us in the past wanted us to go down to the local and have a drink with them on Saturday afternoon. We said we didn't go out on GP weekend, but they insisted, so we met them about 2.30. The pub was very busy, but they had saved us a seat and got us a pint of lager each in plastic glasses. My Margaret smoked long thin cigars in those days. We sat chatting and drinking, and as Margaret had her hand resting on the table, the end of her cigar burnt a small hole in her glass, which obviously she didn't notice. When she went to have a drink, the lager poured out through the hole all down the front of her very light, thin white dress, making it transparent. You could see everything. One of the lads, who was a bit boozy, said, "Margaret, I can see your tits." Margaret just said, "They are clean; also, it's one way to cool down," and she giggled. But when we got up to go, it was worse, as it just clung to her and moulded round her breasts. Margaret just said, "I could be a page three girl now."

As a recreation, we took up short mat bowls. Apart from finding it good fun, we met a lot of lovely people. Also, we started to get very competitive; we got through the county qualifying rounds and became Northants County players. My Margaret was so proud to become a county player. We went on to win over a hundred trophies in Northants, Isle of Wight, and Devon, but the best one was winning the open pairs championship in 1999. My Margaret was so happy, even though she was shattered, and when we got the trophies, she kissed me on the neck and said, "Good night, darling." I turned, gently kissed her, and said, "Yes, my love." I then got a cheeky little giggle from my lovely, happy lady.

We carried on playing league and county, also starting a Silverstone bowls club, playing in the league and competitions. It was great fun, and we got Silverstone on the bowling map, raising money to get mats and such, but we must have upset someone. There was an illegal committee meeting, and we were thrown out. A year later, the club folded, and the equipment that we'd raised the money for was sold. The committee didn't live in Silverstone – I will say no more.

One of our B&B guests who stayed a few times with his lady when they were playing bowls in the area asked me if I had any ideas for a cartoon about bowls I could do for his lady's birthday. Her name was Rose, and this is when Rose Bowl was born. She was a bowl with a rose head and shapely legs in fishnet tights. I framed her and gave it to him; he was over the moon with it.

I visited a printing friend who printed bowls stickers, coasters, and such and showed him a print of Rose Bowl. He thought it was great and said if I could come up with five more ideas, he could make a set of coasters. I said that I would have a go and give him a ring when I had come up with something. On the drive home, Margaret said, "Tel, if you do this, which I know you can, it could lead to quite a lot cartoon work."

I laughed. "We will see," I answered.

"Tel, your little grey cells are working already. I know you, love, when you're excited," she said giggling.

I replied, "Mmm… excited. Good night, darling."

"You just behave yourself," she answered, still giggling.

Yes, I was excited on getting back on the drawing board, and it didn't take me long to come up with Copper Bowl, Fruit Bowl, Pin Bowl, Punch Bowl, and Stone Age Bowl. I finished the artwork and showed them to my Margaret. "Tel, they're marvellous," she said.

We went over to the printer, and he loved them. He said he would get plates made and go into production. They sold well, so to back them up I started doing the woody family; these are based on bowls expressions, like holding wood, chicken wood, so on and so forth. Then, the latest, which Margaret thought were the greatest, were paintings of sayings and films, like Bend it like bowl it like Beckham There's a bowl in my bucket, dear Lisa; Bob the Bowler; old King Bowl; Snow White and the Seven Bowls; and there are a hundred that I did, reduced, and made key rings of.

But just after designing the woody family, my Margaret had a heart attack. The ambulance arrived within minutes after I called it, and Margaret was soon in hospital. After a couple of days, she started to get a lot better, and the doctors were very pleased with her. Seven days later, they let me bring her home, providing that I promised to look after her, to look after my love. "No problem," I told them.

The weeks passed. Every month, I took my Margaret back to the hospital for checks, and every month's was an improvement. Then at last she was discharged; everything was OK. What a great day that was for us both, but I still looked after my Margaret, only letting her do light jobs in the house and a little cooking. My little lady didn't like this, but she knew I was right, so she went along with it. After about a year, she was back to her old self again, but I still insisted that she take things easy, and my lovely little lady agreed.

I was so happy that all was going well and everything was good. But medicinal checks found out that my Margaret was diabetic and had to have three injections a day. Yes, it was a little problem, but I got all the details and gave my love the injections every day, one at 9 a.m. in the morning, one at 6 p.m. in the evening, and a different one at 10 p.m., before she went to bed. Everything was well, and our love got even stronger as we got even closer together, if that was possible. We just loved one another so much. We cuddled and kissed every day, knowing that, as old age was gaining on us, one day things would change, and they did.

As the years passed, my Margaret started to have problems in walking, and had to use a stick and my arm. I got her a try walker to help. At first it upset her and she had a cry, but after a couple of hours she realised what a good thing it was. I cut some wide strips of yellow Fablon and stuck them all along each side of the hall floor as "no parking". This got her giggling again, and I kissed and cuddled her.

Things went well; my Margaret was quite independent now, and we went to bowls practise and league matches. Also, she came with me when I was called to umpire at county games. It was so lovely for her to see all of our bowling friends. Margaret was always happy and laughing despite the pain she had. Also, she watched and coached me with her eyes and hands when I was playing, and at half time had a good talk to me about how the game was going. This was a great help to me. Watching, Margaret could see things that I missed while playing.

Margaret really started coaching me; it was like years ago when she was training me in my Masonic work. She said I was wasted playing lead or two in matches because all the help the England green coach had given me and the CDs he had lent me to study were not being used. "Yes, you're not the best bowler, but you get the best out of your bowlers, as you work very hard skipping them in, not like most skips, who just chat and don't work out a plan or any dangers. You play every wood, yours or your opposition's, and in the last couple of years, when you have been asked to play skip, you haven't lost a match. Think about it, love; you love your bowling, you practise hard, you enjoy it, and you're a hard bloke to beat. Yes, my Margaret was right. I did love my bowling and worked hard at it. I also gave my best when playing for my club and, in past years, in the County with Margaret.

Margaret was beginning to cope well with her frame, and we were still so happy. I was head cook and bottle washer, but my love helped when she could.

Then came what turned out to be the worst day in my life. Just after 7 p.m., Friday, 21 November 2008, my Margaret fell just outside the lounge door. I shot out to find her on the floor in a lot of pain. I told her I would get the chap next door to give me a hand to lift her up. We got her up, but my Margaret was still in a lot of pain, so I rang for an ambulance. On arriving at the hospital, it was found that Margaret had broken her hip.

After a lot of checks and X-rays, it was decided that Margaret would have to go on traction for six weeks. Margaret was very down about this, but I comforted her, saying it would soon go, and I would be in every day without fail to see and sit with her. I also said I would buy some nightdresses for her, as she only wore Calvin Klein in bed. This raised a little smile from her. I leant over and gave her a kiss, and she looked up at me with her big, brown, tearful eyes and said, "Tel. I will never come out of here."

I kissed her again and told her not to be so daft, and I sat with her talking till I had to leave. Getting in my car, I couldn't help thinking of what my Margaret had said. I just couldn't drive, as I was crying my eyes out. It must have been about half an hour before I pulled out of the car park, but I was still crying. as I just couldn't handle the thought of my Margaret not coming out.

Every day, I went into see my Margaret. I combed her hair, checked her nails, took in clean nighties, and made a fuss of her. I tried to keep her happy, but the weeks seemed to drag by. Also, I was concerned that they were not giving her insulin injections at the right times. I complained many times and was told that it was OK.

Six weeks later, great news, I went into see her, and she was sitting at the side of the bed out of traction. I was so happy. I cuddled and kissed her. "At last," I said, "they will have you better in no time at all now."

Margaret then gave me a little smile and said, "Tel, my love, it's going to take a bit longer than you think. The doctor said about six to eight weeks with regular physio." I was a bit disappointed, but I didn't let Margaret see it. I just said it would soon pass.

I still went to see her every day, asking if she had seen the physio and getting the answer no. I was not at all happy, so after thirty days, when Margaret had only seen a physio three times, at seven thirty in the morning, I emailed the hospital patient care department, asking what the hell was going on. At ten thirty the same morning, I got a phone call from them telling me that Margaret was going to be transferred from General to Danetree hospital in Daventry, which caters for older folk that need physio treatment at midday. This was great news – at last, things were starting to move. I was so pleased, but I wish I had complained sooner.

I arrived about one and couldn't have timed it better, for as I parked up, the ambulance with my Margaret arrived. I followed the nurse who was wheeling Margaret up to her room. What a lovely place this hospital was; it was like a five-star hotel. Margaret was taken to a room that had two other ladies, en suite bathroom, and free TV. I put her belongings away in a wardrobe at the side of her bed while they sat Margaret in a chair at the side of her bed. A male nurse then asked Margaret if she'd had any lunch. Margaret's answer was no, so off he went to get some for her. I looked at my Margaret, and she smiled. She looked happier than

I had seen her for a long time. I was so pleased. *This is it now my love is going to get better and will be home soon.*

The sugar nurse came in and said to me that they hadn't sent her night insulin in, but they would send it over by a special car. I said that if I had known I could have brought some up, as I had some in the fridge. Margaret was now eating her lunch that had been brought in, and I was like a cat with two tails. Then the sugar nurse came back in and asked if I could go and get the night insulin from home, as the General had just rung to tell her that they had lost it. I kissed Margaret and said I wouldn't be long.

About an hour later, I was back. By this time, Margaret had finished lunch and was a lot happier, the best I had seen her for a long time. The hospital let me stay for a long while, so we chatted away. When I finally had to leave, I left as a much happier bloke, thinking I would have my love home soon.

The following day, I was there just after ten in the morning, the parking here was great, not like the General, a bloody nightmare. On going into Margaret's room, I saw her sitting by the bed, giving me a smile. It was just fantastic. I went over and kissed her. She seemed in good spirit, but there was a little something that didn't seem right. I thought the work that Margaret had done with the physio before I arrived had made her tired, so I just ignored it.

The nurse came in with a wheelchair to take Margaret down to lunch and said I could go with her. We went into the dining room. It was really nice, and if visitors wanted to have a meal, there was a pay section. As Margaret was eating her meal, I said that tomorrow I would have a meal with her. It was lovely, just like going out for a meal. She gave me a smile, but I still felt she was tired. Also, she didn't eat much. After here meal, Margaret was taken back to her room, and I sat with her for about another half-hour. I thought she needed rest, so I gave her a kiss and said I would see her the same time in the morning. On the way out, I mentioned it to the nurse. She told me that she would check and keep an eye on her, so I thanked the nurse and left, happy but a little worried.

The following morning I was met with a big shock on going in to see my Margaret. She was very ill and didn't even know me. I rushed round to the nurses' station, and the staff nurse said that Margaret had a water infection. They were waiting for an ambulance to take her back to the General. I said, "She just doesn't know me," and I started to break down. The nurse comforted me and told me that the infection does affect the mind, and once they controlled it, she would get better. I sat for a while to sort myself out then thanked the nurses and left. I decided to go home first, have a clean up, then go to the General.

The drive home was hell. I just couldn't stop crying, and on getting to Silverstone, I was quite a state. I stopped at the doctors surgery and went in to see if a doctor would see me and possibly give me something to help. I nearly collapsed. The lady doctor came over and took me into her room and asked me what was the matter. I told her, and she was so understanding and kind. She put her arm round me and explained the water infection problem. She also gave me some tablets I could take at home that would help me, but she said not to drive after taking them. She kept with me until I started to recover. I thanked her, and she said that I was to make an appointment to see her in a couple of days' time, but if there was a problem to get in to see a doctor straight away.

On getting home, I felt quite sick, and I was still weeping. I decided to have a shower and get changed before going to the hospital, as it might make me feel better, but I was so worried about my love.

After arriving at the hospital and waiting about twenty minutes to find a parking place, I went straight to the A&E department. They looked at their chart and told me Margaret had now been transferred to a ward at the other end of the hospital.

I got to the ward early. It was on the first floor, but the nurses wouldn't let me in till it was visiting time, so I had to sit and wait for half an hour. It seemed like hours. At last I got in to see her, but there was no change. I just sat and talked to her, trying to get her to talk to me. Two hours later, I had to leave, but on my way out I had a chat with the staff nurse about Margaret's condition. She told me that it would take at least two or three weeks before Margaret would get over it.

The following day, my Margaret was tiny bit better. As usual, I kissed her and spoke. She looked at me with sad eyes, and I kissed her again and stroked her forehead. She smiled, and I started talking to her. She tried to answer but was having problems, so I asked her just to nod. She did. I said, "I won't be a minute," and went out, as I just couldn't stop crying and I didn't want her to see me like this. I went back in after about ten minutes, took hold of her hand, and started talking to her again. As my Margaret was looking at me, I knew she could see the pain I was in. She tried to squeeze my hand, and I kissed her again and said the hospital would soon have her better and back to Danetree. She smiled, closed her eyes, and started to doze off. As it was nearly leaving time, I kissed her on the forehead and left.

I finally got home, put the car away, and went indoors. I poured a drink and started to cry again. Then I remembered the tablets the doctor had given me, so I took one with another drink and went to bed, hoping to get a good night's sleep.

I continued every day to go in to see my Margaret. She was slowly improving, and I kept talking to her, getting her to answer me, not just nod, making her work, to get my Margaret right again. It was hard, as she got tired. I stroked her forehead, kissed her, and held her hand, trying to comfort her. It was working, for Margaret was beginning to respond. So now, when my time was up and I had to leave, I went to the nurses' station and kept pestering them and asking when my would Margaret be sent back to Danetree. The stall nurse said Margaret was on the waiting list, and once a bed became vacant, Margaret would be sent back there.

It must have been about a month later, I left on my daily trip to the hospital leaving early as usual. I went up to the ward and past the nurses' station to sit down with my book to wait till I could go in and see Margaret. I had been there for about five minutes when the staff nurse came over to me and said that Margaret had been sent back to Danetree, and she was sorry they hadn't phoned me. I was so pleased that I didn't have a go at her; I just said, "Thanks a lot," sarcastically and left for Daventry, mumbling away under my breath.

I drove more slowly than usual, as I was a bit upset that they hadn't rung me. Still, my Margaret was returning to this lovely hospital. I parked up then went up to the first floor to find out where Margaret was. The staff nurse said the doctor was with her and took me to her room. I introduced myself to him to the doctor, and we shook hands. Then he said, "I'm afraid your Margaret has a chest infection."

My heart dropped. *What else can happen to my poor love?* I had to sit down. The staff nurse asked if I was alright and offered a glass of water, as she could see I was distressed. The doctor said he would put her on a inhaling drip to see if it would clear it up. I thanked him, thinking, *What has happened to our lovely world?*

I sat with my Margaret for over two hours, talking to her and holding her hand, but I just don't think Margaret could really understand what was happening. She was dozing on and off, so I kissed her on the cheek and left. On the way out I told the staff nurse I would ring later that evening. It was another hell ride home, trying to drive through the tears. By the time I got home, I was a wreck, shaking, crying, and feeling quite sick.

On getting indoors, I poured a very large brandy, sat down, and tried to sort myself out. I knew I had to eat, but I just couldn't face food. I just sat there, trying to come to terms to what was happening to my lovely Margaret, and for the first time in a long, long while, I went down on my knees and prayed.

I poured myself another brandy, took a sip, put on the coffee table and lay back on the couch. I woke up just after 9 p.m. When I rang the hospital, the staff nurse said there was no change, and Margaret was sleeping peacefully. I thanked her, finished the brandy, made a small cheese sandwich, ate half of it, and went to bed. I was awake at four the following morning with a splitting head, I got up made some coffee and a slice of toast then sat in the lounge thinking of all that had happed in the last six months, trying to convince myself that things must now to start getting better. I had prepared everything for when Margaret would come home: I got special rails to go round the toilet and in the shower and extra rails in the hallway so everything would be OK.

The following day, my Margaret was sent back to the A&E in the General. I sat with her, trying to comfort her, but my love was very ill. She had a mask on and drip tubes in her arms. I kept rubbing her forehead and talking to her. After about three hours, I said that I must pop home but promised her that I would be back that evening. I kissed her on the forehead and left. Again I drove home very slowly, called in at the surgery, and made an appointment to see the lady doctor the following morning in Towcester.

As soon as I got in, I had a glass of water and took some more paracetamols. I been taking these every four hours, as they seemed to help. When my next door neighbour came home from work, I asked him if he would give me a lift in to the hospital that evening, as his dad was in there and he would be going to see him. He said it would be no problem and he would be leaving about seven. I came back and rang the hospital; they told me that my Margaret had been moved to a ward. I thanked them and hung up. I looked at the map I had of the hospital, and this ward wasn't as far as the other one, but I still had a very long walk.

Margaret was a little better but still very poorly. I didn't talk to her too much, as I didn't want to give her too much stress, so I just held her hand and stroked her forehead. When I had to leave, I kissed her said I would see her tomorrow, then kissed her again. She gave me a weak smile. Walking back from the ward, I was very worried and weepy. Seeing how distressed I was, my neighbour comforted me as I got in his car. On getting home, I poured a large brandy and started to think of what Margaret had said a while back – that she would never come out of that place. This really cracked me up, and I was in one hell of a mess. I just couldn't get this out of my mind.

The following day I went in to see my lady doctor. She was so kind, understanding, and helpful; she really knew what I was going through and wanted to see me in a few days' time. That afternoon, I went in to see my love, as I did for the next few days, but she was slowly getting worse. Then my Margaret went into a coma.

On the sixth of March, mid morning, the hospital rang me with the bad news that my Margaret had passed away. I just can't describe what I went through the rest of that day. I knew my life would never ever be the same again, without my love.

Our love for each other was just welded together, never to part. As I'm writing of our life together, I realise what a wonderful life we had together and what a lucky man I was –still am – to have such a lady to be on my arm forever. If any gent out there is reading this book, please, love your lady as much as I love mine, and you will have happiness for the rest of your life. Respect and love her as a wonderful lady, for that is what a lady is, the greatest thing you will hold in your in your arms. Please consider what I'm saying, because if that lovely lady is not with you anymore, it hurts, you're in the pits. Friends I know, I'm there, but I will remain in love with my Margaret forever, as my Margaret.

"Softly Awake My Heart"

About The Author

Terry is a retired 73 year old Artist/Designer who on losing his loving wife felt he wanted to share the wonderful life he had with his Margaret, although he has never written a book before and found it very hard and tearful he done it being pushed on by the lovely memories he has and will never forget.